D0083038

FORMULA FICTION?

Contributions to the Study of Science Fiction and Fantasy
Series Editor: Marshall Tymn

The Mechanical God: Machines in Science Fiction
Thomas P. Dunn and Richard D. Erlich, editors

Comic Tones in Science Fiction: The Art of Compromise with Nature
Donald M. Hassler

FORMULA FICTION?

An Anatomy of American Science Fiction, 1930-1940

FRANK CIOFFI

CONTRIBUTIONS TO THE STUDY OF
SCIENCE FICTION AND FANTASY, NUMBER 3

GREENWOOD PRESS
WESTPORT, CONNECTICUT • LONDON, ENGLAND

Library of Congress Cataloging in Publication Data

Cioffi, Frank.
    Formula fiction?

    (Contributions to the study of science fiction
and fantasy, ISSN 0193-6875 ; no. 3)
    Bibliography: p.
    Includes index.
    1. Science fiction, American—History and criticism.
2. American fiction—20th century—History and criticism.
I. Title. II. Series.
PS374.S35C5   813'.0876'09   . 82-6112
ISBN 0-313-23326-8 (lib. bdg.)   AACR2

Library of Congress Catalog Card Number: 82-6112
ISBN: 0-313-23326-8
ISSN: 0193-6875

First published in 1982

Greenwood Press
A division of Congressional Information Service, Inc.
88 Post Road West
Westport, Connecticut 06881

Printed in the United States of America

10 9 8 7 6 5 4 3 2 1

Contents

Preface

Science fiction, once a haven for a small group of writers and readers, now provides images for a wide and diverse audience. Television, movies, advertising, fiction—both popular and serious—and even theater show the influence of science fiction. Many consider the genre a phenomenon of the last decade, but science fiction fans have known about and read it for over half a century. Why has it become so popular within recent years? Is today's science fiction much different from what fans have read for years? Or has society itself become more receptive to a kind of literature that was heretofore known to only a small coterie?

For answers to these questions, I am looking to the first decade of SF's popularity: the 1930s. During that decade for the first time science fiction flourished, reaching a large audience through the pulp magazines. From one magazine, *Amazing Stories*, which began in 1926 as a showcase for the stories of Edgar Allan Poe, Jules Verne, H. G. Wells, and their imitators, science fiction grew by the 1940s into an enterprise that had a yearly output of one hundred and twenty magazines, forty books, and several Hollywood films. This proliferation occurred as science fiction became distinguished from other adventure-based popular genres (such as detective, romance, and western). Science fiction of the thirties is worthy of close examination because it represents the transition period between SF as a type of adventure and SF as a clearly demarcated body of literature with its own formulas and aesthetic conventions.

Though I discuss significant fiction from *Amazing*, *Wonder*, and *Astounding*, my primary emphasis is on the fiction that appeared in *Astounding*. The most regularly published and popular science fiction magazine of the thirties, *Astounding* produced many stories that have maintained their popularity and remain in print today. In Chapter 1, I briefly describe all SF magazines of the decade and document the centrality of these three science fiction magazines to any study of 1930s science fiction.

The first chapter also discusses those features of thirties SF which identify it with and distinguish it from other types of fiction that appeared in the so-called pulp magazines. SF of the thirties was part of the pulp explosion: 130 to 200 fiction magazines appeared each month in the 1930s. Like other popular genres, SF was available in large quantities, made its money from newsstand sales, fostered new writers, and employed unembellished, often primitive formulas. Yet science fiction distinguished itself from other popular genres because it depicted not society in stasis, but society in flux. I contend that science fiction usually works through juxtaposing a picture of contemporary social reality with a vision of some scientifically explicable change in that reality. The interplay between these two components allows science fiction to comment on social structures and institutions associated with change, progress, and development (in addition to those linked to stability, stasis, and stagnation) in ways other popular forms cannot.

I divide the large amount of SF that appeared in the decade according to its treatment of the relation between these two major components: a picture of 1930s social reality and some scientifically explicable change in that reality. Some of this interaction between a given world and an altered world mimics that found in other popular forms. For example, other genres often show characters in relatively stable situations disrupted by an adventure, a crime, or a love affair in much the same way that the initially static social reality of an SF story is jarred by some chance intervention of a wonder drug, an invasion from another planet, or a miraculous invention. Though much early thirties SF seems directly connected with other popular literature, a large portion of it resembles 1970s SF, and uses formulas that do not resemble those of other popular genres. This literary narrowing-down, this assumption of formulas that employ a major change or anomaly as the organizing principle of the story, suggests more than anything else the appearance and establishment of a new kind of literature.

In Chapter 2 I describe and analyze the kind of science fiction formula that most resembles other popular formulas: "status quo" science fiction. The narrative structure of this formula is fairly straightforward. It opens with a conventional picture of social reality, a picture that could be found in other literature of the day. This reality is disrupted by some anomaly or change—invasion, invention, or atmospheric disturbance, for example—and most of the story involves combating or otherwise dealing with this disruption. At the story's conclusion, the initial reality (the status quo) reasserts itself. This formula clearly has structural ties to other popular forms, but also has aesthetic potentialities unique to it. Its two major elements, "reality" and "change," are of such relative importance and magnitude when compared with the usual focus of popular fiction—the fate of individual characters—that science fiction must be seen in a class by itself.

Status quo science fiction served to affirm existent reality in much the same way that other popular genres of the troubled 1930s affirmed values such as the family, the love ethic, manly heroism, the American Way, and the like. Yet the SF audience must have been a skeptical, disenchanted one. The large quantity and widespread appeal of SF in the thirties suggests that a heroic landscape had lost its credibility for a significant percentage of popular fiction devotees. SF, with its displacement of conflict into an unfamiliar situation, was simultaneously able to offer not only action and adventure but reassurance about the status quo's integrity as well. By removing the adventure to a scientifically plausible realm that, because it was not realistic would not come under close scrutiny, authors of this type of story could depict the triumph of values that in other, less fantastic modes would appear tenuous or outmoded. Though it upholds social values similar to those upheld by other popular forms, status quo SF's displacement of such values suggests that they had begun to lose their currency for many readers.

In Chapter 3 I introduce the "subversive" formula, a variety of SF that comes directly out of the status quo formula and, in fact, closely resembles it. The major difference concerns the relationship between the anomaly and the realistic social setting: in the subversive formula, the anomaly is not expelled, but somehow incorporated into society; in short, society is subverted by it.

This subversive pattern represents a significant movement away from other popular literature formulas. This type of SF focuses on social process: rather than demonstrating how society snaps back to normal after any disruption, subversive science fiction depicts how society adapts to and incorporates the anomalous. The science fictional element is no longer only a technological, alien, or macrocosmic version of a traditional popular-literature conflict. It becomes instead a device that forces the author and the audience to take seriously the kind of change or anomaly introduced, for the anomaly is making an impact on the social structure depicted: altering it, subverting it, destroying it.

The "other world" formula—the subject of Chapter 4— displays no explicit, representational social reality: conventional reality is bypassed altogether in this formula, though it is of course the implied referent for the fictive world. Instead of showing, for example, a string of encounters between aliens and an identifiable agent of known reality (a common mid-thirties structure to be found in both the status quo and subversive tale), a story of the other world type might show a number of slightly confusing pictures of an entirely alien culture culminating in a revelatory scene that suggests some connection to a conventional or familiar reality, thereby reshaping the protagonist's (and reader's) perception of the foregoing events. This formula can also be seen as a variant on the status quo or subversive type which starts from an alternative social reality. The initial "status quo" of this formula is some entirely projected fantastic world, often a version of contemporary social reality or a future evolution of it. Similar in many ways to the recent science fiction of Stanislaw Lem, Philip K. Dick, Ursula LeGuin, and Thomas Disch, this variety emphasizes perception. How should values be formed in the absence of a familiar cultural context? How would our world's values look to complete outsiders?

In the closing section of each of the three main chapters, I evaluate a recent example of each formula. A popular 1970s movie, *Alien*; a work highly honored by SF writers and fans, John Varley's Nebula and Hugo Award winning novella, "The Persistence of Vision"; and several recent stories by writers from England, France, and Poland, are recent examples of the status quo, subversive, and other world formulas that I examine. *Alien* (1979) typifies the expansion of SF out of the pulp magazines and into other popular media. "The Persistence of Vision" (1978), originally appearing in a latter day SF magazine, *Fantasy and Science Fiction,* maintains an explicit connection with its pulp origins. And the short stories (from the early 70s) demonstrate not only how a science fiction formula has been assumed by literary or "mainstream" writers, but also how American SF has influenced foreign science fiction. In the final section of each chapter I offer reasons for the emergence of the SF formula under discussion, and suggest why it has topicality today.

I conclude by assessing the value of 1930s SF, suggesting that its multifariousness alone lends it an importance and identity. The typology of 30s science fiction may be used to identify most subsequent examples of the genre, a fact that illustrates the connection between 30s SF and that being produced today. I argue, too, that such a typology enables the critic to analyze the large, often amorphous body of science fiction and, more importantly, to place it accurately within the matrix of popular and—for want of a better term—serious fiction. Finally, I suggest that this genre emerged because it can offer a look at social processes distinct from (but in a way similar to) that offered by the media: it can dramatize, dislocate, and order events, social processes, and perception in a way that is especially compelling to the media-bombarded, information-saturated modern consciousness, a consciousness that needs not so much relief from the actual, familiar world, as it needs the understanding and perception that a plausible distancing from this world can provide.

1.
The 1930s Pulp Magazines and Science Fiction

INTRODUCTION

Science fiction critics—a relatively new group in literary-critical circles—heatedly disagree about what should be considered the first work of science fiction. Some have cited Lucian as the founder of the genre, while others have named Mary Shelley or Jules Verne. Usually the selection process involves definition-making as well; the works of each "founding father" form the pattern for a new definition of the genre. Indeed, a definition is important, and progenitors are interesting from a historical standpoint. Defining the ancestry of a genre is less important, however, than establishing when science fiction emerged as a distinct kind of literature. The emergence of a genre is a more important phenomenon than the appearance of an isolated writer whose works fail to fit established forms, because this phenomenon requires not only the existence of a group of writers who concurrently want to escape set patterns of literary expression, but the formation of an audience as well. Art responds to changes in society. Determining when a genre that is popular today emerged helps us to define our historical and literary setting and invites us to compare our society with that which produced the genre. But more importantly, the dynamics of the interaction between literature and society can be partially uncovered if those works that comprise the newly emergent genre are analyzed: if the art form is indeed new, it should reflect a certain turn of mind that other literature does not adequately reflect.

Defining the term "science fiction" and looking for the earliest work that fits that definition are only marginally helpful in determining when science fiction writers, editors, and readers realized the genre was to an extent distinct. John G. Cawelti, in *Adventure,*

Mystery, and Romance, points out that "a formulaic pattern will be in existence for a considerable period of time before it is conceived of by its audience and creators as a genre."[1] Early examples, in other words, will actually predate a genre's existence. A definition is needed in order to focus the inquiry, however. Many definitions suffer because they attempt to be so specific that they rule out early works with science fictional elements. A definition should be general enough to include these early science fiction works, but also specific enough to differentiate the genre from other forms of literature. Science fiction's precise relation to utopian fiction, weird fiction, horror stories, and fantasy will inevitably be blurry; in many cases, stories will fit into more than one category. Popular fiction will always have a mix of generic elements in it. Science fiction, for example, will often contain elements of melodrama, mystery, and adventure. But despite this overlapping, a definition can usually suggest at least what is clearly to be included. Detective works must have a detective; westerns require a wilderness setting. That science fiction has invited so many attempts at definition suggests that it extends across a broad spectrum of fictive inquiry.

For the purposes of this study, science fiction is a type of narrative which has as its major element a projected change in environment, technology, or human biology (or any combination of the three).[2] The change is away from the normal, the realistic, the precedented, but is always explicable in a rational, or at least a nonsupernatural manner. The creation of a monster in a laboratory, as in *Frankenstein*, is science fictional, while the unexplained existence of monsters in, say, *Beowulf*, is not. The discovery of another race (a change in sociocultural environment) via scientific expedition, time travel, or alien invasion of earth, is quite different from the postulation of a world in which men exist side by side with elves, dwarfs, and hobbits, as in *Lord of the Rings*. The subject matter—a change of some kind—as well as the attitude toward that subject—rational explanation—determines if a work is science fiction. The genre attempts to show a world operating on the principles of natural laws, with some anomaly inserted. A carefully constructed substitute for these natural laws may be anomaly, but their unexplained suspension is the business of fantasy.

Radical change, of course, has long appeared in other types of literature. Change in environment often constitutes the exciting element of adventure stories, while changes in human biology have long been the staple of Gothic and horror stories. These two types of projected changes are, admittedly, difficult to claim as science fiction's exclusive domain. However, these two types of changes, when accompanied by an attempt at rational explanation, when projected against a backdrop of plausibility and shown as a feature of a world with explicable natural laws, will seldom be found in a non-science fiction story.

Finding early examples of the genre is not too difficult with this definition in hand. Edgar Allan Poe, for example, wrote tales of biological change which had a basis in pseudoscience: "The Facts of the Case of M. Valdemar" examines the effects of hypnosis on the terminally ill patient. H. G. Wells's early works often depict environmental change (of the sociocultural variety) through invasions from Mars or travel to the distant future. H. Rider Haggard and Edgar Rice Burroughs typically show lost or alien races whom adventurers discover in obscure mountain ranges, the center of the earth or, in the works of Burroughs, even on Mars. And Verne's works teem with projected technological change in the form of myriad gadgets and inventions. Much of what these five writers produced is indeed science fiction, but whether their works and those of the writers who imitated them from 1830 to 1930 constitute the emergence of a genre is open to question.

H. Bruce Franklin suggests in his study of nineteenth-century American science fiction that the genre was already well established before 1900.[3] Not only did every major and minor American writer try his hand at the genre, but even the term "scientific fiction" was applied to a type of fiction as early as 1876, in William Henry Rhode's introduction to his anthology entitled *Caxton's Book*.[4] "Whenever the word Romance appears in a title or preface," Franklin explains, "the reader may be sure to find something at least verging on science fiction" (p. xi). Sam Moskowitz writes in *Under the Moons of Mars* (1970) that Bob Davis, the editor of the early twentieth-century magazine *All-Story Weekly*, designated the "pseudo-scientific story" as a brand of fiction that he frequently encountered, and would publish under the rubric of "different story."[5]

These early science fictional stories cannot be viewed as evidence of an emergent genre, however, because they exist more explicitly in other literary modes. Often, for example, they represent attempts at another genre (as Franklin's advice for spotting the early SF story under the code word "romance" implies), slightly offbeat ways of resolving traditional literary problems. Lucian's *True History* falls within the tradition of Menippean satire; Shelley and Poe work in a Gothic/horror mode. Wells's and Verne's works come close to fitting the definition and, to be sure, many of their works have been reissued throughout this century as SF. These writers had acceptable literary "slots" for their works before the 1930s.

Some early twentieth-century stories, now regarded as SF, failed to fit within any traditional mode. Such works were grouped under the term "different story" by Bob Davis, as they were works he found to be "queer, *outré*, unusual, exotic, misfit manuscripts," but which he felt compelled to publish despite their oddity.[6] Like the mutated Gothic/horror/romance, the pseudo-scientific story cannot be ignored as a precursor of modern science fiction. It existed outside the recognized genres, but not self-consciously within a new genre. Taken together, such eccentric fiction constituted the germ of the genre and—in addition to the works of Wells, Verne, and Poe—helped furnish many modern writers with plots and themes for science fiction. Without the emergence of science fiction as a popular and widely influential genre in this century, though, "different stories" would be all but forgotten, disguised by code words, and lumped with all the other eccentric material that has seen print.

Not until the 1930s did science fiction find a secure home as well as an audience through the science fiction pulp magazines. Starting with Hugo Gernsback's publication of *Amazing Stories* in 1926, the science fiction pulps gradually assumed a position of importance in the pulp fiction market. These pulps helped establish a pool of writers who shared a common background and history: American culture of the late 1920s and early 1930s. What before had been isolated stories, curios, or, more often, original ways of approaching fairly traditional literary endeavors, became in the thirties a self-conscious and discrete genre. Though its audience, as David Samuelson suggests, may at first have shared "only the lowest common denominator of fantasies and an ignorance of style,"[7] this audience knew what form these fantasies should take, and professional writers were available in ever-increasing numbers to put them into words. True, the formulas had been there for many years, but finally they had found a historical setting in which they could function as more than mere generic mutations. And it was from this setting—Depression America—that science fiction emerged as a genre.

SCIENCE FICTION FORMULAS

An enormous number of science fiction stories were written and published during the 1930s. And the amount of SF being produced has not declined since—indeed, the late seventies were witness to an upsurge in the production of science fiction. To find the basic underlying structures of the science fiction story, I am examining the first decade of its popularity: the thirties. Not only was this the first decade in which large amounts of SF appeared; it is important, too, because such a wide variety of literature was produced. There was enough variety, I believe, so that almost all science fiction written today can be seen as shaped and anticipated by thirties science fiction. To be sure, there have been some interesting changes in the genre since this formative decade—largely inspired by new discoveries in science—but the basic shape of the fiction was first set forth in the thirties, and I am looking to this period for the start of SF's evolution.

Thirties science fiction would not have been able to attain such popularity were it not related to other popular forms. The parameters of industrial capitalism and specifically of the pulp magazine publishing industry would never allow an entirely new kind of literature to leap wholesale, as it were, from the newsstands: there would have to be a gradual movement into a new genre. The initial period of its appearance would be marked by the publication of other popular literature in only the trappings of the new genre. Indeed, much of the thirties science fiction derived from other genres. War stories, love stories, spy, adventure, detective, horror, air, sea, and sports stories all appeared in science fiction magazines thinly disguised as SF. Gradually, as the decade progressed, this pseudo-SF was winnowed out of the major magazines, such as *Astounding* and the mid-thirties *Wonder,* but still comprised a significant portion of the overall SF production—as it does today. But today's SF of this sort is more cleverly disguised. Nowhere is the connection between popular literature and SF more readily apparent than in the 30s; nowhere are the SF formulas more bare.

If SF could not have emerged without a surface resemblance to other popular genres, neither could it sustain any momentum if it failed to differentiate itself from other widely popular forms, which were, after all, readily available in their undisguised versions. Gernsback demonstrated the unsalability of an SF/detective cross, *Scientific Detective Monthly;* similarly, his *Air Wonder Stories* failed to make any headway. Pure SF, on the other hand, thrived. Popular genres often borrow elements from each other, but to hold a segment of the reading audience, each genre must at least maintain an illusion of singularity.

In addition, the popularity and proliferation of SF in the thirties suggests that it contained easily identifiable and imitable features. These features in popular fiction consist of stock characters (like the hardboiled detective, or the ingénue, or the mad scientist); conventional scenes (the chase, the showdown, the alien invasion); and formulaic, predictable plots. The only originality can be found in the way an author permutes and combines these standard tropes. "Mainstream," or "serious," literature generally resists imitation and replication; the subtle tones, moods, nuances, and multifaceted characters it employs are difficult to describe and define, and even more difficult to imitate. Though certain examples of serious literature will inspire imitation that eventually mushrooms into a popular genre, serious literature does not, as a rule, contain scenes, characters, and plots that have appeared regularly in large numbers of work. Whereas serious literature emerges without easily recognizable antecedents, popular literature seems to feed upon itself.

Finally, the popularity of a large body of literature, or of a genre, implies that it has a connection to social reality. While serious genres—most poetry, for example—can be appreciated on an aesthetic level by a small portion of the population, popular genres have a more widely accessible and familiar metaphor for experience. Science fiction, which started as a fairly small publishing enterprise in the late twenties and early thirties, now makes up a good percentage of all original fiction published yearly in the

United States. The formulas it uses and the metaphors it employs have attained widespread appeal. By analyzing the early evolution of these formulas, the critic can often infer the underlying social features that created the public's need for them. Uncovering such social mechanisms would be a move towards articulating the specifically modern consciousness that has both produced and embraced this genre.

METHODOLOGY

Formula-analysis is the most logical way of sorting thirties SF. Popular literature follows formulas that become apparent after much repetition. By analyzing SF in such a way, by using formula methodology, which has been successfully applied to other popular forms (such as the detective story and popular novel), SF's link with popular literature, as well as its separation from and its straining against formula-bound patterns, can be evaluated.

My major premise in analyzing SF of the thirties is that all science fiction is analogical or mimetic. That is to say, it makes some connection with so-called reality, or it accords with some known way of perceiving the phenomenal world. On the most basic level, of course, science fiction is explicitly linked to culture through the language it employs (perhaps more closely than most SF writers would like to think, judging from the dated dialogue in most older SF). And inasmuch as SF pivots around a central change or anomaly that often appears to be quite removed from daily experience, any analogue—other than language—must, to an extent, be inferred. Such analogues are not difficult to find, however, since most SF stories follow oft-repeated patterns that suggest an overlap with experiential reality. These patterns respond to the concerns of the historical period in which they were created. They embody a shared social consciousness—one, in fact, that readers of the 1980s no longer assume. This picture of social structures which science fiction provides should be the focus of any study of the genre.

Using the term "reality" leads to a set of problems. Does literature ever represent "reality"? Isn't literature always off to one side, as it were, its images always less than shadows of any real world? For the science fiction critic, the problem becomes:

how is the sentence, "John opened the door to his house and looked out on the three suns above the planet Frak" any more or less realistic than "John opened his back door and called his children in from play"? Both sentences are about imaginary characters (whom I just invented), so the truth value of each should be the same. Both are written in English, though an unusual proper noun can be found in the first—a proper noun which could easily be omitted. The images the two sentences conjure up for me, however, differentiate them: the first conjures an alien world; the second conjures up a mundane and realistic one. The second suggests, for me, a status quo. To be sure, much of the world a story suggests is merely that inferred by the reader, and some readers will infer different kinds of worlds than others. Science fiction writers today often blend seemingly normal, everyday events with the anomalies in their stories, consciously creating friction through the interaction. But in the 1930s, science fiction writers were less sophisticated, and actually took pains to make the two portions of their stories (anomaly and reality) discrete and easily identifiable. While this is not the place to speculate on the degree to which literature reflects or stands for or imitates reality— important issues—I can state with some confidence that most science fiction sets up a contrast between the anomalous and the real, making identification of the component parts a fairly simple matter.

One objection to the "analogical" view of SF is that writers would have explicitly written about "Reality" in more or less straightforward terms if that indeed had been their main interest. That is, using a science fictional superstructure to discuss everyday social issues appears to be a rather roundabout fictive strategy. It seems, for example, that there would be better ways to comment on race relations than by depicting a war involving earth, Mars, and Jupiter (as many SF writers chose to do in their stories in the 1930s). In fact, social messages often seem tacked on. For this reason, many critics have been reluctant to take SF seriously.

Once a science fiction story can be shown to evoke a specific social reality, once its masquerade is, in a sense, penetrated, the problem remains to establish a convincing link between the anomaly and reality. The usual methodological approach draws out themes from the SF at hand—alien invasion, inventions, artificial life forms—and shows how such themes comment on current issues by extrapolating them into a possible future. How an invasion story reflects world power struggles, how an invention story comments on technological potentialities, what commentary an artificial life story makes about scientists experimenting with protoplasm, are all strategies the theme-school of SF criticism might employ. Such a critical stance is bound, of course, by the themes it looks for, and usually ends up denying the fictional nature of the works at hand. The SF it criticizes therefore transforms into speculative futurist tracts, a metamorphosis that does damage to the literature. The critic needs, instead, a way to discuss the theme (or anomaly) an SF story centers on as well as a method of evaluating the entire work within a larger aesthetic framework. Only by looking at the work as a whole, with other science fiction as a background, can the presentation of a seemingly autonomous, unreal world be plumbed and connected with the world of its writer and readers.

The structural approach used here takes both of these difficulties—epistemological (why reality is conveyed in other-worldly terms) and methodological (how to determine what comment on social reality SF makes)—into account. I am seeking to uncover the overall patterns of SF that appear after having been repeated by different writers time after time. Instead of using theme as the organizing principle of SF criticism, I am offering "formula" or "narrative structure" as the element most crucial to categorizing, differentiating, and analyzing SF stories. The terms of the formula are as follows: mimesis (the portion of the narrative in which the experiential, realistic, quotidian world of the writer is evoked); anomaly (the unprecedented but logical changes introduced into this world—the element that makes a story SF); conflict; resolution; and authorial stance. By breaking down SF into these elements, the major conflict—mimesis versus anomaly—is thrust into the foreground in such a way that both the fictive and the real world elements hold equal weight.

Such a critical stance helps solve the critical problems because the importance of theme is devalued. SF emerges not as a way to represent static reality, but as a way to metaphorically delineate society in flux, or social process. The other-worldly terms and the aura of plausibility combine to make statements about a world not-our-own which operates in comprehensible ways. The processes of this other world usually reveal the author's conception of social dynamics in his own society.

The three basic patterns are what I call the "status quo," the "subversive," and the "other world" forms of SF. The status quo story moves in a straightforward way: conventional reality is disrupted by change or anomaly of some kind, but by the story's end the conventional order has reasserted itself. The subversive story also starts with a traditional picture of experiential reality into which an anomaly is introduced. But instead of depicting the expulsion of the anomaly, the subversive story shows society adapting (or crumbling) in response to it. The other world structure radically departs, as might be expected, from any specific (or even slightly veiled) depiction of the author's social/experiential milieu; its terms and events are almost entirely removed from the identifiably naturalistic. This is the most mature variant of SF formulas and appears with regularity only toward the end of the 1930s. There are variants on each of the formulas, of course, but these three basic structures form the foundation for American SF during and since the 1930s.

Several features of short stories need to be isolated when attempting to differentiate and analyze them through formula-analysis. The nature of the overtly depicted reality, for example, carries considerable weight. A change or anomaly will clash with this real-world element, so the fictive strategies authors employ to depict reality will be fairly standardized: they want to make clear what is the reality and what the anomaly. I am looking not only for the conventional and quantifiable ways this reality is embodied (the family unit, the hero, the locale, the particular local conflict, the social class that seems to be the focus) but also for the author's stance on these matters. SF is a remarkably multifarious genre; two stories on the same theme with a similar mimetic element can suggest entirely different things. In one, the author can be demonstrating the strength and independence of our social structure, while in another, the social structure's intrinsic weakness and resistance to change may be stressed. Much of this authorial stance, too, must be gleaned from a view of the story as a whole— not just from a glance at its initial depiction of reality. By combining the picture of static reality with the social process implied by the story's conflicts and resolutions, the critic can infer the author's sense of a real-world-based social environment.

The nonreality, or the anomaly, carries equal weight. In a formalistic sense, this anomaly functions as a literary device for carrying the story along. In most SF, it functions as a hinging-point for the central conflict. Its importance in determining the overall structure and format of the story varies widely; occasionally a story will use this anomalous element only as a background to a character study; sometimes it will overshadow not only character, but plot line as well. One way of determining its centrality is by looking at the anomaly itself and deciding to what extent the story could work without it. Few can. The anomaly determines the narrative structure of most SF.

This anomaly's plausibility elevates science fiction out of fantasy, and into a realm where it must be taken seriously. The way the anomaly first appears and how characters react to it help determine its plausibility. The critic need not, however, make explicit connections between the story's anomaly and actual current events. That is, the state of biological experimentation has little to do directly with the fictive portrayal of such experimentation in SF; stories about space travel depend in no direct way upon the actual exploration of space. These stories need not be scientifically accurate and up-to-date, nor even predictive, nor even seriously evaluative of scientific issues. Instead, the stories intend to suggest an aura of plausible reality. Such an aura sufficiently removes the events from the actual, from existent space/time locales, yet at the same time keeps the fiction grounded in a known logical system. Such a displacement strategy accomplishes two things. First, it removes the events and the society depicted in a story to so-to-speak neutral grounds, a political-social arena not charged by expectation and prejudice. Second, this strategy acts as a verification device. By maintaining in the story logical systems and explanations based on our own science/culture, comments made about social process, interaction of character, and the like count for something and are matters of some importance to the reader. It is not all wild conjecture, for example, to write today about races of clones or cyborg creatures: stories on these themes have a connection to current events. But these creatures are not yet here; hence, any story about them must imply a removal from strictly naturalistic settings. Stories about them have enough grounding in our reality to maintain a nonfantastic mode but enough distance from the real to estrange the reader from relevant fact and opinions. Many SF stories, then, evince a genuine freedom of expression: The social processes they imply can be taken seriously because the stories deal with issues close enough to those in our own realm. Yet, the seriousness takes on an added dimension because the reader's prejudices have been neatly neutralized by the SF mode. Issues can then be examined under a new, clean—if alien—light.

Perhaps more importantly, this displacement strategy works on the SF author as well as on the reader. Where the reader can abandon preconceptions and be seduced, in a sense, by a science fictional removal or coverup, the author is equally estranged from any compulsion to make real-world connections. Along with the construction of the patently (but plausibly) nonreal, the SF feels endure and transcend specific venues. The events themselves are amimetic, but the way in which they interact and have effects on characters—both of which are, in SF, subservient to known systems of logic—demonstrates an implied view of social workings and dynamics; murmuring beneath the operation of the nonreal is the author's social consciousness. Much of the social content in SF is purposefully placed in the story, but the better SF does not overtly and consciously refer to a specific reality. Rather, it convincingly projects an imagined world whose connections to our own are only oblique. The author of this type of story does not write allegory, but lets social meanings emerge from his story in an inferential way.

This view of SF's effect on the reader and the creative process allows a straightforward and understandable methodology for the SF critic. Aside from the formalistic considerations mentioned above—which are more descriptive than analytical—the main thrust of the SF criticism I am proposing is to show what sort of social process emerges from a particular story or group of stories. Various themes will suggest various social dynamics, but once placed within one of the three formulas, the story can be seen and evaluated against others like it. Extrinsic considerations and connections to specific social events are important, and will be noted in passing, but the focus of the methodology used here will be discovering what the fiction itself suggests, separate from its surrounding social/historical milieu, and what breakdown of the formula is necessary before meaningful statements can be made about the fiction.

The main and most important relationship within a science fiction story is between social experiential reality, as the author's audience would have accepted it, and the stated anomaly. The first, most obvious level of analysis concerns acceptance of the anomaly by characters within the story: is the anomaly valuable or repulsive, good or bad, useful or destructive? In two of the three SF formulas (the status quo and the subversive) there is always a genuine attempt at mimesis, so the interaction between the real world and the anomaly can be easily ascertained. In the third formula, however, the anomaly's general utility *vis-á-vis* experiential reality has to be inferred from the author's stance. This initial judgment of the new, anomalous values or forces in light of the old, empirical reality makes for a great deal of the tension and suspense in most SF stories. It also sets up major premises. When the Martians invade earth in H. G. Wells's *War of the Worlds,* they are indisputably evil. There is no compensating knowledge or benefit to be associated with their visit; the anomaly is absolutely repulsive. Any criticism of the novel must start with this fact, and statements about the novel's meaning will necessarily spring from the initial question of what earth can (or should) do in the face of such unmitigated evil. Analysis of any SF story must first take the anomalous elements at the level at which the story itself deals with them, and proceed from there to more complex issues of meaning and importance.

After the initial reaction of experiential reality to the anomaly is discerned—either in the story itself or through the author's stance—the reader distances him/herself (with the author) one more degree from the story, and determines whether that reaction is right or wrong. Many stories show, for example, a society rejecting a race of aliens, an invention, or some other anomaly when such a change clearly could provide something useful and valuable to the society. Likewise, society is sometimes shown embracing anomalies that will bring about chaos, destruction, and despair. Many SF stories use dramatic irony to show things about society and groups that these societies or groups themselves cannot see but which are manifestly clear to the reader. And all these ironies and levels of discourse must be sorted through by the SF critic; in an attempt to uncover the precise relation of society to the anomaly an archeological process must be followed. What the anomaly suggests about society is often difficult to determine. So, too, the segment of experiential reality displayed often fails to align itself with identifiable real-world analogues, but the relationship between the two—the society as presented by the story, and the author's view of it—can usually be determined.

One way to uncover a story's implied version of social process is to examine the fate of people and groups revealed simultaneously with this central science fictional (that is, anomaly-reality) relationship. Often a fairly traditional "real world" conflict will provide the framework for the story's events. For example, a story will open with a situation in which a man and a woman want to get married, but the woman's father neither likes nor trusts the man. In more traditional forms such a story would probably move on to show confrontations between the man and the woman's father, attempts by the man to prove himself, and the like. In SF, though, a frequently repeated story line is one in which the man, in an effort to prove his mettle, submits to the father's experiments. These experiments carry the man into the fifth dimension, to the moon, under the sea, to the center of the earth, to prehistoric times, or to any other conceivable (anomalous) locale. The major focus of the story, comprising perhaps 90 percent of the text, will then be the heroic efforts the man makes to escape from this bizarre realm. Perhaps the father and daughter will get themselves involved in the other-worldly excitement, and the man will save one or both of them. The story usually concludes with the man—having proven himself—marrying the woman. Many later stories do, of course, become more subtle, interesting, and complex, but a "human interest" subplot usually surrounds the SF element, and leads the reader to the locus of values that underlies the action. What in a more usual genre would be entirely passé, conventional, or outmoded, can often appear in a science fiction story—veiled or obstructed by an anomaly—as the major driving element.

In this instance, the anomaly only serves to highlight the "proving" process the suitor must undergo. It works as a metaphorical version of the social process in which a man must, to an extent, defer to his fiancée's father. The aura of plausibility (the father's research experiments) serves not so much as a way to comment on the use of human subjects, nor as speculation about space/time/dimensional traveling, but as a means of authenticating the social structure and the travails it involves. The scientific, nearly plausible terms lend a dimension of seriousness to what would ordinarily be considered a fairly trivial matter. A banal plot can therefore be given weight—or publishability—by injection of terms and situations ordinarily associated with serious, important matters.

Were the anomaly, contrarily, not surrounded by scientific plausibility, were it, say, achieved by a witch casting a spell on the man, or a demon intervening in the man's life, an entirely different set of associations would emerge. Where the scientific terms gravitate toward encompassing all society and suggest a typicality or repeatability of situation, fantasy terms would suggest an individuality or singularity, and would thrust the story into an entirely new realm—that of the supernatural. Many of Thorne Smith's novels, such as *Topper* (1926), *Turnabout* (1931), and *Rain in the Doorway* (1933), employ science-fictional themes (invisibility, transference of souls, parallel worlds), but bypass any attempt at plausibility. Indeed, the idea of a demon casting a spell on a man is no more probable than that of a scientist inventing a time machine—they are both rather farfetched. Rather, the context that surrounds the situation, either a scientific, wide-ranging world view or a supernatural, eccentric one, should be carefully evaluated when interpreting the story.

This ur-text, it should be noted, is of the status quo variety, which tends to affirm existent reality, and is inherently less speculative and more politically conservative than other SF formulas. The subversive and other world formulas, which appeared more toward the end of the decade and especially since the thirties, are more complex in the ways they depict social processes, and in the ways they set up scientifically based obstructions or dislocations. In addition, they resemble other popular forms less overtly than does the status quo formula, which recalls, for example, traditional adventure and horror structures. As SF grew in popularity, these SF-specific formulas emerged with it. The ways these later formulas describe and comment on social processes are more difficult to elucidate, too, particularly since they never evoke a naturalistic version of reality. The general methodology brought to bear on all SF formulas will essentially be the same archeological procedure, though: uncovering component parts (anomaly, reality, authorial stance) and looking for relationships among them that suggest meaning.

THE PULPS

Science fiction of the thirties has never been adequately analyzed— or even described—because most of it appeared in pulp magazines. Robert Scholes and Eric Rabkin dismiss thirties science fiction under the title "A Pulpy America";[8] Brian Aldiss attributes the major science fiction of the thirties to Kafka, Stapledon, and Huxley.[9] Darko Suvin summarily dismisses the American science fiction that appeared between the wars.[10] To be sure, the pulp magazines are difficult to take seriously today. Not only were there an enormous number of them, but specifics concerning their publication, circulation, and even authors are very difficult to find. It is widely assumed that 30s science fiction shared many pulp conventions. In terms of publication processes and, in fact, story lines and characters, it did. But the model of shoddy, hastily composed truckloads of fiction designed for uneducated masses not only fails when applied to all science fiction in the pulps, but fails in its application to much of the other pulp literature as well.

There was a certain stigma attached to reading the pulps, much less studying them. Many contemporary analyses reflect this stigma, and distance themselves from the subject. Others over-compensate and fervently laud the pulp magazines. The truth about the 130-odd pulp magazines which appeared throughout the thirties is cloaked by their reputation as trashy escapist literature. And, as part of that pulp tradition, thirties science fiction has been routinely overlooked and misunderstood as well.

The pulp magazines, usually 7" by 10" in size, 120-144 pages long, and printed on unfinished "pulp" paper—hence the name— came into being when Frank Munsey printed *Argosy* on rough stock paper in the early 1890s.[11] The late 1920s, the 1930s, and the early 1940s saw their rise and proliferation. Those who did not experience this period first-hand are incapable of gauging the sheer magnitude of pulp magazine selling. Even those who lived through the era were often oblivious to the pulps, inured to the sight of their bright covers adorning newsstands. It took an outsider, Aldous Huxley, to vividly portray the extent of the pulp magazine's place in America. Writing in 1937, Huxley explains his experience in a northern Florida town:

> In the main street alone I found no less than six shops devoted to the sale of nothing else than periodical pulp. From the brilliantly lighted windows scores and hundreds of highly colored female faces, either floating in the void, or else attached to female figures in a partial state of undress, gazed out from the covers of magazines. Sometimes there would be rows and rows of the same face. More often, however, taking pride in the extent of his stock, the shopkeeper would build up whole picture galleries, in which every head was different. In one window I counted upwards of eighty separate publications, each one with its own yearning or saucy belle.[12]

Huxley's response to America in general seems to have colored his assessment of the pulp magazines, but his testimony bears witness to the enormity and variety of pulps for sale.

The number of readers of the pulps has never been precisely determined. Magazines were not required to print circulation figures (as they are today), so circulations could only be estimated, even at the time. An approximate figure for pulp magazine circulation of the mid-thirties is ten million—and since most magazines were read by at least three people, it can be fairly guessed that the pulps were read by thirty to forty percent of the literate American public.[13] As with the number of titles available, the uncertainty about circulation figures reflects the general tawdriness that surrounded the pulps. They were mass-produced fiction for the masses, and if a title did not fulfill its proper economic function—circulating to large enough numbers—it would fold almost immediately. Although precise figures for circulation, readership, and even number of titles will never be available, it seems clear that there was a market of considerable size for the pulp publishers' wares.

The contents of the pulp magazines are less difficult to assess. Generally, there were four large classes: adventure, western, detective, and love stories. Commentators from the thirties divide them in differing ways, depending on their particular emphasis and viewpoint. Huxley, for example, sees most pulps as having some relation to pornography, while Archer Jones, an academic writer of the thirties, sees more variety to the pulp market. *The Writer's Handbook* of 1940 divides the pulps into Romance and Confessions; General Adventure; Air, War, and Spy stories; Detective and Mystery stories; Fact Detective stories; Scientific, Weird, and Supernatural; and Westerns—seven categories. Suffice it to say that the fiction published in the pulps spanned a wide range of genres, but that generalizations about their contents have proven problematic.

Because the number, circulation, and even the contents of the pulp magazine are difficult to determine, its status is naturally relegated to unimportance. Very few critics of the thirties were sufficiently interested in the pulps to do a close analysis of them; too, the canon changed with extraordinary abruptness and apparent whimsy. To most, they were a "throwaway" fiction that acted as anodyne for the masses during a time of great social unrest. It did not so much matter how many there were, or how many people read them, nor what they contained. They were assessed instead by the way their stories were composed. Henry Morton Robinson, writing in *Bookman* in 1928, sets the tone for the following decade's commentary on the pulps in his article entitled "The Wood-Pulp Racket." There is no art to the pulps, he maintains, no lasting virtue—only monotonously repetitious formula fiction. There are "no library file copies of wood pulp," he concludes.[14] Yet the criticisms of the following decade struck a less ironic note as the pulp industry survived and thrived during the Depression. Archer Jones assesses the pulp writer's self-image: "His aspirations and rewards are those of the businessman, not the artist. Painful experience has taught him that he is but the amanuensis of the machine."[15] Fletcher Pratt notes a similar mechanicalness to the writing of pulp fiction. A friend of his who wrote for the pulps sold the same story, "altering nothing but the names and a few rods of description . . . to a western, a gangster, a world war, and a supernatural pulp in succession."[16] But perhaps the most striking evidence of all supporting criticism of the way pulp magazines were written is made by an anonymous pulp writer. His complaint concerns the kind of effect writing large quantities of pulp fiction has on the writer himself: "It is working oneself into this alien mood, this primitive emotional and cerebral pattern, that poisons the brain like a drug, atrophies the perspective, and dulls the spirit."[17] Since pulp writers were paid by the word, they sought, naturally, to produce large quantities of fiction. And the production of such large quantities had an effect on both the writers who were responsible for producing it and on the commentators who sought to define it.

Harold Hersey, having edited both pulp magazines and what he refers to as their "sisters under the skin: the smooth paper magazines,"[18] defends the quality of pulp writing: "I can unhesitatingly say that the average professional pulp writer is easily on a par with the average 'smoothie' " (p. 127). It is significant that an editor of both types of magazine would so baldly level distinctions between the kinds of writing each produces. That the overwhelmingly obvious features of pulp fiction—its immense quantity, its imitativeness, its mechanical production, the rough paper upon which it was printed—can be set aside by Hersey suggests an attitude about the fiction that might prove useful: it can indeed be considered separately from the way it was produced and from the kinds of stock formulas it followed. Writing formula fiction for quick sale to low budget magazines is not perforce a worthless enterprise. Indeed, if 130 "slick fiction" magazines appeared every month, it is likely that certain formulas used in their stories would also become abundantly clear.

Generally, the thirties critics felt that the pulps could only be justified by the fact that they employed thousands of people when jobs were scarce. *Time* pointed out the range of people who benefited from the pulp magazine industry in 1935: "Distributors, wholesalers, dealers, second-hand stores, literary agents, typewriter and ink manufacturers, mail-order advertisers, wastepaper dealers and the Salvation Army all drew liberal support from the pulp press."[19] Archer Jones's generally negative view of the pulp magazines is in fact tempered only by an assessment of their importance as economic stimulators. Presumably any activity that generated jobs and money—and was ostensibly within the law— was respected in the thirties. If the magazines could help America out of the Depression, then they were laudable; but if they wasted valuable time, money, and energy, they were not. The fiction they produced was quite beside the point.

Today's assessment of the pulps is scarcely more searching. Robert Kenneth Jones prefaces his analysis of the "weird menace" pulps with this remark: "There's little social significance to the stories that form the framework of this study."[20] He goes on to point out that they were "churned out" for readers needing a "quick escape" and marketed by firms looking for a "quick sale." Such extrinsic factors need not necessarily preclude social significance, though, and do not excuse the critic from doing more than merely summarizing the magazines' contents. Robert Kenneth Jones goes on to state that an unnamed pulp writer told him, "I don't strive for social content," an admission that, while no doubt perfectly honest, should not be regarded as a definitive statement on pulp writing. Charles Beaumont similarly dismisses the pulps from serious critical attention. "Happily," he writes, "no sober, critical evaluation of the pulps is possible. Like any other narcotic, they defy rational analysis. One can speak of their effects, even of their ingredients, but not—without wearisome and unconvincing pomposity—of their causes."[21] Finally, Beaumont, like Robert Kenneth Jones, fails to offer a critical, close analysis, but offers in its stead the nostalgic reminiscence that much current discussion about the pulps seems to generate. Like Jones's interpretation, which stands as a justification for the summaries that comprise his book, Beaumont's shying away from "sober, critical evaluation" allows him to use the pulps as a springboard for fond recollection.

Judging from the criticism written on the pulps, they are a form of popular literature that is widely misunderstood. No study (other than Archer Jones's) has ever been attempted on the pulps, nor have they attracted much passing commentary. It seems unusual that an industry which provided the American public with enormous amounts of reading material should be completely ignored today. It suggests, in fact, that there are major reasons it is ignored: large obstacles standing in the way of research, or ideological biases that are difficult to overcome.

Perhaps the most overwhelming reason so little has been written on the pulps, though, is that they have been completely superseded today. The feeling that a new movement entirely encompasses and in a way negates and subsumes its predecessor is particularly strong with the pulps, probably because the magazines physically disappeared so abruptly with the coming of World War II, and were quickly reincarnated in newer, flashier forms—paperbacks, comic books, television. The SF magazines today are a small industry by comparison with SF books, television shows, or movie productions. The pulps do survive in reprints—consider Dashiell Hammett, Erle Stanley Gardner, Raymond Chandler, the *Doc Savage* books, *The Shadow,* and the multitude of science fiction stories of the thirties on the market—but in formats that have a greater feel of permanence to them (books), or that convey an appropriate ethereality (television and movies). So the originals, difficult to remember, obtain, understand, and preserve, have been replaced, repackaged. And these replacements have been so thoroughly pigeonholed and assimilated by our society that their previous existence is almost negated: repackaging the past to a certain extent expunges its reality.

SCIENCE FICTION IN THE PULPS

While most other pulps disappeared by the 1940s, the science fiction magazines survived.[22] Indeed, the genre seemed to continue its late thirties momentum: twelve new titles appeared in the forties.[23] The science fiction pulps offered something that could not be found in other formats; the metaphor for experience they provided was so unprecedented and immediate that the genre could survive even in an outmoded format. This extension of the pulp science fiction magazine's active life well beyond that of the other pulp magazines reflects on the first full decade of science fiction pulp production—the 1930s—suggesting, perhaps, that science fiction pulps also had a uniqueness when they first appeared. Unlike the other pulps, the science fiction magazines had as their subject not so much a particular body of specialized knowledge— all the accoutrements, complete with language, artifacts, and characters, of one specific subculture (the cowboy, the detective, the aviator, the spy, and the ingénue are figures around which other pulp fiction revolves)—as a way of perceiving the world that cut across all such superficial features of subcultures. What started in the thirties as another fictive entrance into a new culture hero's milieu (the scientist's), ended the decade as an assessment of how the scientific perception of reality was affecting American society as a whole.

Taking cultural change as its subject matter required the science fiction pulps to adopt a tone that differed significantly from that of the other pulps. Thomas Uzzell outlines what he considers the typical contents of a love pulp as well as what kinds of appeal each story strove for: a rich-girl story (meant to provide the reader with vicarious thrills); a poor-girl story (a "Cinderella" situation many readers could project themselves into); a Hollywood or radio story ("behind-the-scenes" glamor); and a story about a "hero in uniform."[24] The science fiction pulps took a much broader vision of life, what might be called—considering the social atmosphere in which they appeared—a more "realistic" angle. They fall, for the most part, outside of Archer Jones's description of the pulps as a "mirror to yearning." Bernard DeVoto stresses the difference: "The science fiction pulps have something like uniqueness. . . . the popularity of doom in pulp paper, is as striking a portent as you will find anywhere in literature. . . . These stories crudely express the phantasies that oppress us all, which are not fermented in paranoia but merely reasoned from any day's headlines."[25] Though it would be wrong to suggest that all thirties science fiction stories had as their central action the destruction of mankind (or its salvation), the genre nonetheless permitted and fostered such speculation, which lent it a certain distinction.

Though they were often professionals who also wrote for other pulp magazines, the science fiction pulp writers had at their core a group who perceived themselves to be purveyors of a new kind of fiction. Jack Williamson, a prominent contributor to the thirties pulps who is still active today, writes: "I think we had a feeling of belonging to a new culture, though we wouldn't have put it that way. . . . we were amateur futurologists aware that . . . we were sometimes exploring alternative future tracks of human history. That was an exciting privilege."[26] Such a self-image contrasts markedly with that of the anonymous pulp writer whose "A Penny A Word" appeared in *American Mercury* (see note 16) and who bemoaned the "alien mood" required to write for the pulps.

As an economic enterprise, writing for the SF pulps was more questionable—or perhaps more courageous—than writing in other pulp genres. At the start of the thirties there were only three markets for stories: *Amazing, Astounding,* and *Wonder.* Turning a rejected science fiction story into one that could be sold to another type of pulp magazine was hard, often bootless, labor. The early thirties stories were frequently didactic, filled with ponderous pseudoscientific explanations. It was a type of story that was relatively fixed by its genre. DeVoto remarks, "They fulfill the hopeless dream of detective story writers: they are a kind of fiction in which explanation is action."[27] Unfortunately for writers, pseudoscientific explanation is not so easily transformable into love-explanation or western-explanation. Harry Bates, editor of *Astounding* from 1930 to 1933, claims that he had to accept a great many inappropriate manuscripts for his magazine because he did not want to discourage and lose potential contributors. "Where else might they sell a story that I had turned down?"[28] The early science fiction magazines, then, were filled with curious stories: ones by professionals that perhaps did not quite fit the genre as it existed, and stories by new writers who were interested —perhaps obsessively interested—in writing only science fiction.

It is the latter group of young, enthusiastic, idealistic science fiction writers who helped the genre find a place for itself in the mainstream of American life. Like Williamson, who was excited at the prospect of doing something new and exceptional, these writers worked to appear in print more regularly by the mid-thirties. Bates remarks that by 1933 there was "an almost sufficient body of somewhat worn writers and a just-emerging group of fresh, young, potent, potential writers, all of them fan-condensate."[29] John W. Campbell, editor of *Astounding* from 1938 until his death in 1971, substantiates Bates's claim: "Most of the writers who made their first appearance before 1940 were under twenty-five— a number of them in their teens. (Myself, for instance.)"[30] And, not surprisingly, these science fiction pulp writers made considerably less money at their trade than did masters of other pulp genres. Frederick Faust earned about one hundred thousand dollars a year writing as "Max Brand," and Erle Stanley Gardner reputedly

earned about seventy-five thousand dollars each year.[31] Eando
Binder, making about thirty-five hundred dollars a year, was
probably the best paid science fiction pulp writer of the era.[32]
In short, science fiction writers only wrote partly for the money.
They also wrote because they enjoyed it, or felt themselves to be
fulfilling a larger purpose. That much of what they wrote rose
above the standard pulp formulas is not altogether surprising.

The science fiction pulp, like all others, made its money not from
subsidies, promotions, subscriptions, or advertising; virtually all its
profits came from newsstand sales.[33] For this reason, more than any
other, the pulp editors had to satisfy their audience. And the
difficulty with pleasing them was that they were almost impossible
to assess. Editors developed a keen anxiety concerning the readers'
makeups, personalities, and tastes. Harold Hersey, editor of many
pulp magazines, gives an inventively metaphoric description of the
editor's relationship to his reader:

> It is this fiction reader, first and last, who makes the final
> decision; this abiogenetic moster of the natural born editor's
> imagination . . . who only comes to life by a slow, painful
> process in the average editorial brain. . . . Gradually,
> inevitably, if he stays in the profession, the editor constructs
> the entire character of his reader much as a paleontologist
> reconstructs a prehistoric animal from fossilized remains . . .
> he finally gets the wobbly, lifeless, reconstructed creature
> known as The Average Reader to his feet. In some secret,
> unexpected moment it breathes and moves. The danger now
> is that it may become a Frankenstein monster. It lumbers
> after him from then on wherever he goes, haunting his sleep
> and whining its endless monotonous criticism of everything
> he does.[34]

Though decidedly light in tone, Hersey's remarks illustrate the
analytical/projective process reader assessment involved, and the
heavy psychic investment editors made in undertaking it. The
editor, through a trial and error process, attempted to determine
what pleased his audiences most. There were no intervening con-
glomerates to shape policy, no large advertisers whom editors had
to be careful not to offend, no huge marketing departments to

promote the literary product. Hence the audience had a great deal to do with what was turned out on the printed page: it helped—in an oblique way—to edit the fiction.

The larger pulp audience, an audience from which the more specific readership of science fiction was gradually distinguished over the course of the decade, has been assessed in almost unanimously negative terms. Archer Jones contends that though Theodore Roosevelt, Woodrow Wilson, and Herbert Hoover were pulp readers, "the average reader is a dissatisfied man of twenty-eight with an infinite capacity for wishing."[35] Thomas Uzzell's picture of the average love-pulp reader delineated a similar individual whose only difference from Jones's is gender, "women whose lives are cast into a world of dull routines—factory girls, housewives, domestics, shop-girls, office workers."[36] Though much was made within the pulp ranks of the multitude of professionals who read the pulps, the average reader was most certainly not a doctor, lawyer, or senator.[37] On the other hand, the first pulp editor whom Alvin Barclay worked with in the twenties (but whom he does not name) is incorrect in labeling his reader "The Great American Moron"; the magazines had a wide appeal.[38]

The science fiction audience must have been in some significant ways very different from the audience of the general pulp magazine. DeVoto remarks, "Whoever they are, something more than the need to escape must take them to their reading—and something more than mere satiation with the two-gun sheriff and the blonde who is never quite seduced."[39] Quentin Reynolds remarks in his history of the publishing house of Street and Smith that *Astounding* had high sales in black neighborhoods such as Harlem and the south side of Chicago.[40] Reynolds suggests that science fiction appealed to blacks because the stories' contents were removed from earth struggles, ostensibly transcending religious and racial boundaries.

The most significant development from the audience of science fiction pulp readers was the "fan." The true science fiction enthusiast, the fan was a reader who became deeply involved in all kinds of activities extending beyond the perusal of the science fiction pulps and centering around the discussion of SF stories. F. Orlin Tremaine, editor of *Astounding* from 1933 to 1937, comments in a September, 1934 editorial: "There is something

about the readers of *Astounding Stories* that is a little different
from any magazine group. It's more intimate, closer, with a clearly
defined kinship of common interests."[41] The true fan sought to
establish something of the community Tremaine alludes to. And,
of course, the more "true fans" the editors could locate, the more
magazines they could sell. Hugo Gernsback, who founded *Amazing
Stories* in 1926, played a large part in helping science fiction
readers become aware of each other. He ran pictures of the oldest
and youngest readers, held slogan contests and contests to design
a logo for the magazine, and carried a letters column that printed
the full names and addresses of the correspondents. He even ran
a contest for which readers submitted essays entitled "What am I
doing to popularize science fiction?"[42] It is true that the fans
were young and eccentric. In his history of forties fandom, Harry
Warner estimates the average age of the fan as twenty;[43] Damon
Knight depicts all early science fiction fans as people with gross
physical deformities—obviously an exaggeration to support his
contention that science fiction fans were extraordinary individuals.[44]
The fans formed into clubs, printed amateur magazines (an early
letter-writer to *Astounding* calls for others to band with him and
create an "ideal science fiction magazine"[45]), established ideologies
inflammatory enough to cause "wars" among them, and invented
a language of science fiction fandom that had enough consistency
to be used in the fan magazines.[46]

Though these active, even fanatic, science fiction consumers
comprised only a small portion of the science fiction audience,
their effects on the genre were far-reaching. They helped spotlight
science fiction as a genre with commercial possibilities and great
importance to an (admittedly small) group of people's lives.
The first science fiction fan convention, which took place in New
York in 1939, received write-ups in *Time* and *The New Yorker*;
the small presses that fans created to print books (Arkham House,
Shasta, Fantasy Press, etc.) showed major publishers that there
was a market for science fiction.[47] It was the core group of active
fans and the large group of readers (estimated at 150,000 per
magazine in 1939 by *Time*[48]) who helped make science fiction a
clearly defined social/economic enterprise by the close of the
decade; they created for it an extrinsic support structure the
public at large could appreciate.

It is less difficult to get a sense of the fan audience and the pulp publishing industry that surrounded—and to a certain extent controlled—science fiction's rise in the thirties, than it is to effectively focus on a set body of literature that can be said to be representative of thirties science fiction. An enormous number of stories were published in the science fiction magazines—probably about four thousand in all—and at least a score of hardback books appeared each year as well. A number of well-known science fiction/horror films came out in the decade, which ended with Orson Welles's radio production of *War of the Worlds.* "Literary" science fiction works, such as Aldous Huxley's *Brave New World* and Olaf Stapledon's *Last and First Men*, as well as a number of highly popular "scientific romances" by authors such as Edgar Rice Burroughs and A. Merritt, provided competition for the science fiction pulps. Yet the largest volume of science fiction appeared in the pulp magazines. And though it must always ground itself in the surrounding social and literary climates, any study of thirties science fiction must focus on these pulps. Through them the genre was introduced to a wide readership, and in their pages most of the formulas developed which still shape science fiction today.

Rather than sampling all thirteen science fiction magazines of the thirties, I have decided that an in-depth study of just one, *Astounding Stories,* will prove to be most useful. Though *Amazing Stories* and *Wonder Stories* published notable fiction at times—especially in the early thirties—*Astounding*'s late thirties fiction has proven to be of more lasting value. Its fiction has been that most widely anthologized since the thirties, and much of it still remains in print today. (See Table 1, which summarizes the fiction of importance these three magazines printed.)

Astounding recommends itself on other levels as well. It was published by Clayton Publishers from 1930 to 1933 and by Street and Smith from 1933 to the decade's close. Being issued by such large companies gave *Astounding* a firmer financial base than that enjoyed by the other magazines and enabled the editors to pay writers consistently and generously. Fan literature abounds with accounts of Hugo Gernsback's unscrupulous editing policies at *Amazing* and *Wonder* (which he edited after losing *Amazing* through financial difficulties); he would regularly fail to pay

Table 1 The Important Science Fiction Pulps of the Thirties

	PUBLICATION DATES	EDITOR	SIGNIFICANT AUTHORS	PUBLISHER
AMAZING	1926-29	Hugo Gernsback	H. G. Wells, Jules Verne, Edgar Allan Poe, A. Merritt, Murray Leinster, Phil Nowlan[a]	Hugo Gernsback
	1929-33	T. O'Conor Sloane	Jack Williamson, E. E. Smith, P. Schuyler Miller, Otis Atelbert Kline, David H. Keller, Edmond Hamilton, Raymond Z. Gallun, John W. Campbell, Stanton A. Coblentz	Teck Publications
ASTOUNDING	1930-33	Harry Bates	Arthur Burks, Ray Cummings, Victor Rousseau, Nat Schachner, Murray Leinster, Arthur Leo Zagat,[b] Edmond Hamilton, Jack Williamson	Clayton Publications
	1933-37	F. Orlin Tremaine	Raymond Z. Gallun, Stanton A. Coblentz, John W. Campbell, Clark Ashton Smith, Stanley G. Weinbaum, John Taine, C. L. Moore, H. P. Lovecraft, Willy Ley, E. E. Smith	Street and Smith
	1937-40	John W. Campbell	The Tremaine "stable," and Robert E. Heinlein, Isaac Asimov, A. E. Van Vogt, L. Sprague deCamp, Lester del Rey, Clifford Simak, Theodore Sturgeon, Henry Kuttner, L. Ron Hubbard	Street and Smith
WONDER	1930-34	Hugo Gernsback (through 1933, David Lasser; 1934, Charles Hornig)	Clark Ashton Smith, John W. Campbell, Clifford Simak, John Wyndham, Jack Williamson, Stanley G. Weinbaum, P. Schuyler Miller, Laurence Manning, David H. Keller, Edmond Hamilton, Eando Binder	Hugo Gernsback

[a]With the exception of Nowlan, the stories printed by these authors were reprints.
[b]The first six authors here are writers who had been successful in writing pulp fiction for the general magazines before they came to *Astounding*.

writers for their stories, or pay them less than the agreed-upon sum, or pay them only after they threatened him with litigation. Bates, Tremaine, and Campbell, the editors of *Astounding* in the thirties, have never been cited for such breaches of ethics. By all accounts, *Astounding* also had the largest circulation of any of the science fiction pulps in the mid-thirties through the forties; to publish in it guaranteed not only payment, but the widest readership as well.

Perhaps the most compelling reason *Astounding* can be taken to be representative of the science fiction pulps, though, is that it was the first to take science fiction seriously as a genre. Gernsback's *Amazing,* first appearing in 1926, four years prior to the first issue of *Astounding,* consisted largely of French, German, and English reprints—Verne, Poe, Wells, and their imitators. It was a backward-looking enterprise that, while quickly attaining a circulation of one hundred thousand, rapidly exhausted its resources when it attempted to carry into the thirties its tradition of ignoring the work of American professionals. *Astounding,* by contrast, immediately engaged the professional pulp writers whose work resembled science fiction, paid them well, and established a steady, reliable market for fiction of similar quality and emphasis.

It is not surprising, then, that the editorial stance *Astounding* adopted differed widely from that of its early thirties competitors, *Amazing* and *Wonder.* Gernsback's policy of instruction, as stated in an early issue of *Amazing,* was one he carried into his thirties *Wonder* (and which his former employee T. O'Conor Sloane continued in the early thirties *Amazing*):

> Not only do these amazing tales make tremendously interesting reading—they are also always instructive. They supply knowledge that we might not otherwise obtain—and they supply it in a very palatable form. For the best of these modern writers of scientifiction have the knack of imparting knowledge, and even inspiration, without once making us aware that we are being taught.[49]

This policy raised two problems: few writers existed who wrote fiction of this sort, and writers who strove to incorporate instruction and information into their fiction had trouble doing so without being tedious.

Harry Bates, the first editor of *Astounding,* had a significantly different policy. Michael Ashley points out that the contributors to the first issue of *Astounding* (with the exception of S. P. Meek) were authors who had been writing for Frank Munsey's magazines (*All-Story, Argosy,* and so on).[50] Though the magazine's title was *Astounding Stories of Super Science,* the writers were actually experienced veterans of adventure fiction. Bates himself remarks that the elements of action and adventure were very important to *Astounding,* but notes that he had difficulty in finding appropriate stories:

> We [Clayton and Bates] could think of fewer than half a dozen fair-to-good pulp writers who had ever written stories of the kind we wanted, but we never doubted that some of my adventure writers could produce them. . . . [But] most of them were almost wholly ignorant of science and technology, so much of what eventually got put into their stories in one way or another had to be put there by myself. . . . I did very much rewriting.[51]

Harry Bates's sense of science fiction was so clear that he would alter stories to fit his preconceived notions. What differentiated Bates's idea of science fiction so markedly from Gernsback's, however, was the connection Bates maintained with a fictive genre of the past: adventure fiction. Where Gernsback's *Amazing* and *Wonder* sprang from his earlier factual magazines, *Electrical Experimenter* and *Science and Invention,* Bates's emerged from the tradition of popular fiction.

F. Orlin Tremaine, *Astounding*'s first editor at Street and Smith (the publishing house that acquired *Astounding* in late 1933), brought a great deal of pulp editing experience to what Bates calls "a small but healthy *Astounding.*"[52] After an initial period of experimentation printing fantasy and "weird" fiction, Tremaine discovered what would separate his magazine from his competitors': the "thought-variant" story. Though Campbell later continued this idea with his "mutant" stories, Tremaine must be credited with its inception. Instead of using science fiction as a way to instruct, or as a variety of the supernatural tale, Tremaine sought to connect the fiction he printed with the scientific changes in society: "Our purpose is to bring you each month one story carrying a new and unexplored 'thought-variant' in the field of scientific fiction . . . it opens the way for real discussion, discussion deeply connected with social science, the present condition of the world, and the future."[53] His editorials (and editing) differed widely from those of the mid-thirties *Amazing,* which would print (in place of editorials) strictly factual articles by its editor, T. O'Conor Sloane, an octagenarian who held a Ph.D. in chemistry. Add to this independent editorial stance Tremaine's policy of ignoring "name" writers and reading all the submissions himself, and the reasons for *Astounding* flourishing in the mid-thirties become abundantly clear.[54]

The third editor of· *Astounding* in the 1930s was John W. Campbell, Jr. (1910-71). A science fiction writer of some stature himself and an assistant of Tremaine, Campbell enlarged Tremaine's theories of science fiction and put together a stable of extremely competent authors which included many writers who are still active today.[55] Campbell stressed the social commentary science fiction could provide, as well as the climate of current scientific work it should acknowledge. He wrote in June, 1938, of the difference between scientific fact and fiction: "Fact differs from fiction in this; science fiction presents all those things suddenly, fact requires a generation of improvement and change to attain the practical, useful article. And by that time, we have become accustomed to the idea, accept it so readily and naturally as to see no particular advance."[56] In the same editorial, he stated with conviction his feeling that "the discoverer of atomic power is alive on earth today." Unlike the editors he competed against in the late thirties (Ray Palmer of *Amazing* and Leo Marguiles of Popular Publications), Campbell was constantly aware of science fiction's place in society, and *Astounding*'s mission to establish that place. He wrote in March, 1938, "We are adding '*science*' to our title, for the man who is interested in science must be interested in the future, and appreciate that the old order not only does change, but *must* change."[57] The stories he printed, therefore, had a different slant than those of his competitors and predecessors. Campbell considered himself something of a social reformer who had under his power the magazine most attuned to social speculation; though he has been criticized at times for being overprescriptive in his editing, he was, nonetheless, the profession's first futurologist.

Ray Palmer of *Amazing,* and Leo Marguiles, editor of *Thrilling Wonder Stories, Startling Stories, Captain Future,* and a number of other pulps, envisioned science fiction as a far less serious enterprise. Palmer appealed frankly to a "fringe" group—"People," Jack Williamson writes, "not enlightened enough to tell the difference between crude fiction and actual fact."[58] W. S. Baring-Gould cites a fan magazine that describes *Amazing*'s audience as a "semi-religious group," believers in pyramidology, Lemuria, Mu, Atlantis, and the like.[59] Marguiles seems to have rivaled Palmer in cynicism. At the first world science fiction convention in 1939, Will Sykora, a particularly fervid fan, announced publicly, "Let us all work to see that the things we read in science fiction become realities." Marguiles is alleged to have responded: "I am astonished. I didn't think you boys could be so damn sincere."[60] Apparently, Marguiles's conception of his subject and audience was vastly different from that of the *Astounding* editors. His plan for *Captain Future* was straightforwardly formulaic, having little to do with social or scientific change. Sam Moskowitz recalls the formula: "There must be a superscientist hero. There must also be aides: a robot and an android and, of course, a beautiful female assistant. Each story must be a crusade to bring to justice an arch villain; and in each novel, the hero must be captured and escape three times."[61] By the decade's close, *Astounding* had captured for itself a market of serious science fiction readers that other magazines could never match.

I should note two things here about the sampling technique I am using. First, short stories and novellas are being used because they are easier to discuss in their entirety and because, generally speaking, they tend to be more unified and more focused than novels of the period. Many of the SF novels of the thirties were simply expanded versions of stories that originally appeared in pulp magazines and thus were no more significant than the stories. Even today, much of the SF being produced suffers from its length; it is a rare SF novel that can sustain its momentum to the end. And it is even rarer when a science fiction novel can remain entirely focused within the boundaries of SF formulas without taking off into some other, recognizable popular format such as the detective story, romance, or adventure tale. Second, a small number of stories will be used to represent the types and variations of thirties SF formulas. From this small group, it is hoped that a much larger body of fiction—both diachronically and synchronically—can be understood. Although those stories I pick are representative, "pure" examples of discrete formulas that usually tend to blend into one another, the formulas have nonetheless appeared a great number of times before, during, and since the thirties. Some stories discussed here have recently been reprinted, but this is less striking than the enormous number and variety of stories that fulfill the conditions of each formula.

NOTES

1. John G. Cawelti, *Adventure, Mystery, and Romance* (Chicago: Univ. of Chicago Press, 1976), p. 8.

2. Environment is a broad classification in itself, including both the physical environment and sociocultural environment, the latter including the influence of other cultures.

3. H. Bruce Franklin, *Future Perfect* (New York: Oxford Univ. Press, 1966), p. x.

4. Franklin, p. xii. Subsequent references will be inserted in the text.

5. Sam Moskowitz, *Under the Moons of Mars* (New York: Holt, Rinehart, and Winston, 1970), p. 402.

6. Moskowitz, p. 402.

7. David Samuelson, "The Spinning Galaxy: A Shift in Perspective on Magazine Science Fiction," *Extrapolation,* 17, No. 1 (Dec. 1975), 47.

8. Robert Scholes and Eric S. Rabkin, *Science Fiction: History—Science—Vision* (New York: Oxford Univ. Press, 1977), p. 35.

9. Brian Aldiss, *Billion Year Spree* (New York: Doubleday, 1973), pp. 181-208.

10. Darko Suvin, *Metamorphoses of Science Fiction* (New Haven: Yale Univ. Press, 1979), p. 9. Later, however, Suvin remarks that U.S. SF of the 1930s, while excluded from his study, is nonetheless worthy of study (p. 205).

11. Theodore Peterson, *Magazines in the Twentieth Century* (Urbana: Univ. of Illinois Press, 1956), p. 283. He cites the birth date of the pulp magazine as 1896.

12. Aldous Huxley, "Pulp," *Saturday Review of Literature,* 9 (July 17, 1937), 10.

13. Interpolated from statistics found in *Historical Statistics of the United States, Part 1* (Washington, D.C.: U.S. Dept. of Commerce, 1975), p. 8; and *Statistical Abstract of the United States: 1977* (Washington, D.C.: U.S. Dept. of Commerce, 1977), p. 138.

14. Henry Morton Robinson, "The Wood-Pulp Racket," *Bookman,* 67 (August 1928), 651.

15. Archer Jones, "The Pulps—A Mirror to Yearning," *North American Review,* 246, No. 1 (Autumn 1938), 44.

16. Fletcher Pratt, "The Pulp Magazine," *Saturday Review of Literature,* 17 (July 3, 1937), 4.

17. "A Penny A Word," *American Mercury,* 37 (March 1936), 292.

18. Harold Hersey, *Pulpwood Editor* (New York: Frederick A. Stokes, 1937), p. 10. Subsequent references will be inserted in the text.

19. "Pulp Pride," *Time,* 26 (Sept. 16, 1935), 33.

20. Robert Kenneth Jones, *The Shudder Pulps* (West Linn, Oregon: FAX, 1975), p. xiv.

21. Charles Beaumont, "The Bloody Pulps," *Playboy* (Sept. 1962), rpt. in *The Fantastic Pulps,* ed. Peter Haining (1976; rpt. New York: Vintage, 1976), p. 399.

22. Beaumont, p. 412.

23. Michael Ashley, *The History of the Science Fiction Magazine: Vol. 2, 1936-1945* (Chicago: Regnery, 1976), pp. 201-2; and *Vol. 3, 1946-1955* (Chicago: Contemporary Books, 1977), pp. 323-25.

24. Thomas Uzzell, "The Love Pulps," *Scribner's,* 103 (April 1938), 29.

25. Bernard DeVoto, "Doom Beyond Jupiter," *Harper's,* 179 (Sept. 1939), 448.

26. Jack Williamson, "The Years of Wonder," in Thomas Clareson, ed., *Voices of the Future* (Bowling Green: Bowling Green Popular Press, 1976), p. 3.

27. DeVoto, p. 446.

28. Harry Bates, "To Begin," in Alva Rogers, *A Requiem for Astounding* (Chicago: Advent, 1964), p. xiv.

29. Bates, p. xvi.

30. John W. Campbell, "Letter from the Editor," in Rogers,p. xxi.

31. "Big Business in Pulp Thrillers," *Literary Digest,* 123 (Jan. 23, 1937), 30.

32. Angela Gibbs, "Onward and Upward with the Arts: Inertium, Neutronium, Chromalogy, P-P-P-Proot!" *New Yorker,* Feb. 13, 1943, p. 48. Originally cited in *Literary Digest.*

33. Archer Jones maintains that the pulps made less than 10 percent of their profits from advertisements.

34. Hersey, p. 66.

35. Archer Jones, p. 36.

36. Uzzell, p. 41.

37. "Pulp Pride," p. 33.

38. Alvin Barclay, "Magazines for Morons," *The New Republic,* Aug. 28, 1929, p. 42.

39. DeVoto, p. 448.

40. Quentin Reynolds, *The Fiction Factory* (New York: Random House, 1955), p. 257.

41. F. Orlin Tremaine, "Editor's Page," *Astounding Stories,* Sept. 1934, p. 150.

42. Sam Moskowitz, *The Immortal Storm* (1954; rpt. Westport, Conn.: Hyperion, 1974), pp. 5-10.

43. Harry Warner, *All Our Yesterdays* (Chicago: Advent, 1969), p. 25.

44. Damon Knight, *The Futurians* (New York: John Day, 1977), pp. 3-8.

45. "The Readers' Corner," *Astounding Stories,* Mar., 1931, p. 442.

46. There have been four full-length studies of science fiction fandom: Moskowitz, Warner, and Knight (cited in previous notes), and Beverly Friend, "The Science Fiction Fan Cult," Diss. Northwestern University, 1974.

47. David A. Randall, Sigmund Casey Fredericks, and Tim Mitchell, "An Exhibition on Science Fiction and Fantasy" (Bloomington, Ind.: Univ. Office of Publications, 1975), p. 33.

48. "Amazing! Astounding!" *Time,* 34 (July 10, 1939), 32.

49. Michael Ashley, *The History of the Science Fiction Magazine: Vol. 1, 1926-1935* (Chicago: Regnery, 1976), p. 23. "Scientifiction" was the term Gernsback used to refer to the scientifically oriented fiction that he printed.

50. Ashley, Vol. 1, p. 33.

51. Bates, pp. xii-xiv.

52. Bates, p. xvi.

53. "Let's Get Down to Brass Tacks," *Astounding Stories,* Dec. 1933, p. 139.

54. Frank Gruber, *The Pulp Jungle* (New York: Sherbourne Press, 1967), p. 90.

55. Among these were Robert Heinlein, Isaac Asimov, A. E. Van Vogt, L. Sprague deCamp, Lester del Rey, Clifford D. Simak, Jack Williamson, Henry Kuttner, and Theodore Sturgeon. For comparisons to other pulp magazines, please refer to Table 1.

56. John W. Campbell, Jr., Editorial, *Astounding Stories,* June 1938, p. 21.

57. John W. Campbell, Jr., Editorial, *Astounding Stories,* Mar. 1938, p. 37.

58. Williamson, p. 7.

59. William S. Baring-Gould, "Little Superman, What Now?" *Harper's* 193 (Sept. 1946), 286.

60. "Amazing! Astounding!" p. 32.

61. Cited in Ron Goulart, *An Informal History of the Pulp Magazines* (1972; rpt. New York: Ace Books, 1973), p. 169.

2.
Status Quo Science Fiction

The science fiction found in the thirties pulp magazines that most resembles other popular formulas I am labeling "status quo" science fiction. The narrative structure of this formula is fairly straightforward: it opens with a conventional picture of reality, a picture that could be found in other popular literatures of the day. This reality is disrupted by some anomaly or change—invasion, invention, and atmospheric disturbance are some examples—and most of the story involves combating or otherwise dealing with this disruption. At the story's conclusion, the initial reality reasserts itself. Such a structure clearly has ties with other popular forms. It uses a device that only temporarily supplants or challenges the order of this world; it always maintains a connection to this world; it depicts characters who are generally stereotypical, and who exist largely as vehicles for the formula's fulfillment.

Such a formula, though in a sense bound by its connection with older popular forms, also has aesthetic possibilities that suggest a breaking off from older forms and a lack of interchangeability with them. The status quo structure, for example, frequently works against its apparent "roots": often it not only questions the surrounding social reality, but fails to depict it in a strictly representational way at all. Some stories, about invasions from space that are repulsed by earth, show scientists having direct access to the authorities. Others, about remarkable inventions, depict an immediate acceptance of these inventions by the populace. In short, these early stories often depict the world as the authors and the readers might have wanted it to be, but in a way which both groups realized was very far from the truth of the matter.

Not surprisingly, the same writers who simplify and distort the reality they depict eventually establish new formulas to work through, and new varieties of the status quo structure itself. For example, the "inverted" status quo formula appears fairly regularly throughout the thirties. Society is shown expelling the anomaly or change in this formula, too, but it is deemed foolish or flawed for doing so, because the anomaly is a positive, beneficial one. Another variety of the status quo tale, the "transplanted" status quo, depicts familiar, workaday characters in unusual, science fiction-like (even fantastic) circumstances (deep in space, at the center of the earth, etc.) from the very beginning. There is no initial picture of the everyday world. In these settings the characters encounter the very anomalous, the extremely alien, which they expel. Stories of this type are usually recognizable by the conventionality of the values and relationships among the inhabitants of the "transplanted reality," and by the disappearance of the strangeness of this transplantation once the anomaly is encountered. For example, the spaceship setting of a story in this category may first appear quite futuristic and the crew's lifestyle exotic, but after the crew on board the spaceship is somehow transported to another dimension, the initial "transplantation" seems only minimal.

Throughout the thirties, the status quo formula seemed both to embody and transcend the more traditional popular forms. This structure must have looked familiar to avid readers of pulp magazines. The "classic detective story" (as defined by John G. Cawelti) takes a similar structure. Into a fairly conventional and familiar world a crime intrudes, and by the story's conclusion, the crime is solved, and the integrity of society is reinforced.

> The intrusion of the outside world on the serene and reflective calm of the detective bachelor's establishment was elaborated by Conan Doyle into the memorable scenes at 221B Baker Street. . . . The crime symbolizes not only an infraction of the law but a disruption of the normal order of society. It is something extraordinary that must be solved in order to restore the harmonious mood of the charming scene by the blazing fireplace.[1]

It even more closely resembles the "fantastic journey" variety of adventure story: the protagonist of a central group of characters journeys into the unknown or the forbidden but safely returns to the comforting, familiar world by the end of the story. Horror stories often exhibit a similar structure. The horror element is introduced into a conventional world (or sometimes arises through placement of conventional types in a horror setting such as a haunted house) and causes excitement, chills, and thrills; but finally the real world reasserts itself and order reigns.

Throughout the following discussion, the connection between this status quo formula and other popular literature will be shown, but the stress will be on how essentially different this formula is from other popular formulas. The difference stems largely from the possibilities science fiction can open up. Such possibilities revolve around the existence of the anomaly (or the SF element), that feature in science fiction that is found in no other popular form. Usually the longest and most carefully constructed part of the story, this anomaly has developed out of some antecedent conflict or action in the first part of the story, and thus maintains a connection to the familiar world. It may be the artificial life form that a scientist has worked all his life to create. But this anomaly distinguishes SF, even that employing the simple status quo formula, which is most connected with popular formulas, helping it become a unique literary enterprise.

THE SIMPLE STATUS QUO STORY

The simple status quo structure, most common at the opening of the thirties, but evident throughout the decade (and still doing service today) is a fairly straightforward distillation of the structure mentioned above. A reality that is entirely familiar to the reader confronts the anomalous and triumphs over it. The simple status quo tale is one in which the unprecedented is expelled or is swallowed up, as it were, by the larger, more powerful existent social structures. Some early pulp SF writers who used this formula—Arthur J. Burks, Captain S. P. Meek, Murray Leinster, Ray Cummings, Victor Rousseau, and Victor Endersby—were successful pulp writers in non-SF magazines. They quickly saw the financial rewards for hurriedly recasting adventure tales in SF terms. Not entirely uncreative, though, they saw the potentialities the SF element carried; their works should not be ignored altogether. These writers not only helped to establish a pattern that many younger writers followed and played against, but they also lent the endeavor an aura of professionalism that went a long way in helping SF to establish itself.

An ur-text follows with my gloss interspersed. This text is formed by looking for conventional plots, heroes, conflicts, and anomalies which appear in large numbers of stories but only rarely appear all at once in any one tale. The ur-text, then, is a composite picture of the most oft-repeated and conventional features of a formula. The patterns and formulas, it should be remembered, are such that they allow for individual creativity: each story is at once formula-bound and singular, working at once with and against the basic pattern. The ur-text, however, is entirely conventional, containing more clichés than a writer would ever be able to sell in one story. Conversely, no story would be able to sell without at least a good portion of these ur-textual features.

Things are uneventful, indolent. Perhaps it is a lazy, tired period: "The year of Grace 1935! A dull year, a comfortable year!"[2] People go about their business in a routine way: "Louis Sparth rowed ashore from his schooner unhurriedly, with easy strokes. He always liked to take his time with pleasant things."[3] There is a real stasis here, and against this (often only implied) background of static reality, various characters appear who seem to be restive, driven, or obsessive—or who are sometimes simply the pawns of chance—on whom the action will focus. More often than not, the main character will be a "hero-type" of the kind usually associated with adolescent literature. Successful in many phases of endeavor, he is young, brilliant (often in scientific work), unmarried. Seldom, it should be noted, is this main character a woman. Seldom is the hero either stupid or very poor. He is rather like a Horatio Alger protagonist in an intermediate stage between rags and riches. Wealth and some social status are usually accessible to him (or were accessible to him at one time) because these accoutrements increase possibility, and the early part of the story must brim with the possible, the potential adventure. The inertia accrues until it reaches critical mass; then the story moves into its second phase. And the more conventional the first part is, the greater the shock of anomaly.

Onto this comfortable familiarity disruption descends. This disruption can take many forms: a breakthrough occurs in the laboratory; a freakish discovery is made by a scientific expedition; contact is established with a faraway planet. In early 30s stories, the disruption often results from happenstance; a meteor falls; a letter or telegram arrives: " 'That's why I sent for you, Allan,' he said quietly. 'To go to Mars with us tonight.' ' "[4] The familiar world of the first part crumbles almost entirely at this stage. The story focuses instead on the anomalous circumstances—the civilization found under the sea, the dangers of another planet, or the like. Even late 30s stories employing this status quo formula make only a bare pretext of an explanation in order to plunge the main character into the anomalous: James Cardew is exiled to Jupiter in Thornton Ayre's "Penal World" because "he knew too much of corruption in high places."[5] Paul Ernst's "The 32nd of May" (*AS*, April 1935) epitomizes the kind of change or anomaly SF protagonists find themselves subject to: The narrator, visiting some friends, is abruptly thrust into "a soundless, motionless world of gray, with geometric masses rooting in a plane made of some firm, rubbery substance no more like the ground we know than air is like iron."[6] The change can be effected in many different ways; but generally, the more severe the dislocation, the more dramatic the struggle against it, and the more heroic the act that is needed to overcome it.

The struggle between the agent of known reality and the anomaly can take many forms. Ordinarily, two main conflicts operate in the status quo story. First, the values, ethics, or morals embodied by the agent of reality (usually the hero) are suddenly thrust into a world in which they no longer matter. A new morality, therefore, is at least implied—particularly since survival usually ranks of paramount importance—and it always works against the known, accepted, fairly conservative values the hero embodies. He must do any number of things to save himself—kill, bribe, appear nude before or sleep beside women he does not know. Such actions flout the codes and rules he has always lived by, but are accepted actions when he finds himself among aliens, immersed in the bizarre. A second moral conflict involves the alien force's actions. They know no ethical restrictions or guidelines, or at least they don't obey ours. The evil scientist in Douglas Drew's "Nightmare Island" (*AS*, Oct. 1936), Peter Wolfe, has abandoned ethical standards entirely. "Wolfe carried [a woman's] limp body across the laboratory and laid it upon the broad stump of the Tapan, then, after amputating her feet at the ankles, set the shin bones deep into the sap wood."[7] This plant-animal union grows for a few weeks. Soon Wolfe "fashioned a whip and came to stand beside her. 'Open your eyes'. . . . he lashed her twice, three times" (p. 122). All sorts of taboos, such as unfettered sexuality, polygamy, homosexuality, sadomasochism, incest, bestiality, cannibalism, human sacrifice, torture, and genocide, can be carried on by agents of the anomaly. Readers could devour such fare with no sense of guilt or shame because the underlying message is always the reassuring one that this behavior is wrong, the product of creatures or cultures entirely removed from the human realm. The reader could be comfortable knowing not only that such actions are being condemned, but that they are the ones that the agent of the familiar world actively works to defeat.

The classic response to this anomaly is expulsion. Accomplished by a variety of means, the danger is averted, and the familiar world reestablishes itself at the story's conclusion. The scientific method often establishes the real hero. When the world is threatened by another planet's proximity in John D. Clark's "Minus Planet" (AS, April 1937), James Carter (the hero) "reached for a dozen reference books, a slide rule, and a wad of paper, and immediately became oblivious to all about him."[8] Conventional values work to actively oust or abandon the anomaly: pertinacity, self-awareness, love, loyalty, patriotism. Usually, opposition to the anomaly is deliberate, though in some status quo tales a certain amount of luck is involved. And this expulsion of the anomaly is usually presented as the correct response, too. The themes that such stories center on—invasion, evil aliens, awful biologies, destructive technologies—generally threaten society. The reassertion of "reality" at the story's conclusion—no matter how it is effected—is accepted as essentially the best resolution to what was potentially an enormously threatening chain of events. In short, status quo stories usually have happy endings.

This reassertion of conventional reality and all its concomitant mores is enacted not only through the actual abandonment/destruction/expulsion of the anomaly, but through the pleasing resolution of the fates of individual characters as well. Tom

Curry's story, "From an Amber Block" (*AS*, July 1930), tells of some paleontologists who discover a living, dangerous creature inside a fossil. The creature is killed, and at the end the main character remarks, "To the devil with paleontology, Betty. You saved my life. Come out and let's get married. I love you."[9] Since so much of the action involves proving oneself, or maintaining acceptable ethics in the face of the unknown, characters are forced by outside circumstances to show their true worth. And the good—those who maintain accepted, real-world standards and values—usually reap rewards at a story's conclusion; the bad usually receive their just deserts.

The aesthetic value of such a structure may appear limited. An author has apparently very little room for creativity or inventiveness. It seems odd, too, that so many writers and readers were attracted (and continue to be attracted) to such a predictable pattern. Indeed, the limitations of this story pattern must have been evident to readers and writers, inasmuch as the writers used many variations of the formula and several new formulas gained popular acceptance.

Yet there are a number of ways the status quo formula avoids being a simple reenactment of one well-worn, conventional plotline. Any established popular formula (and even by the early thirties the status quo one was well-known to readers of popular fiction) always operates against the background of what it could conceivably be. That is, nonfulfillment of the formula or fulfillment of a contrary formula is—in the better stories—always threatened or imminent. In the status quo SF story, for example, the anomaly introduced could come very close to wreaking havoc; or reality could be so grossly altered that it would no longer be recognizable. John Russell Fearn's story, "The Brain of Light" (*AS*, May 1934), concerns a war between earth and the "Light Beings." The latter become enraged when a new radio and television system interferes with their universe (which coexists with our own). They retaliate by sapping all color from our world—it becomes black and white—and then by sapping light altogether. A war ensues between the Light Beings and the human race, and the aliens are defeated, but not before they deploy weapons which project color at humans and drive them mad, which turn earth unnatural hues, and the like. Fearn uses a similar strategy in "The Man Who Stopped the Dust" (*AS*, March 1934), a story detailing the results of an experiment that rids a major city of all dust particles. Like other skilled authors working within the status quo format, Fearn pushes to extremes the extent to which reality is distorted and nearly destroyed; the extraordinarily inventive near-destruction his stories depict elevates them above the common run of routine, formula-bound fiction.

Status quo formula stories can bypass a tedious conventionality through their depiction of social taboos. One of the major conflicts in all status quo tales, the tension between accepted values and those encountered through anomaly, can be accentuated by having accepted values very nearly flouted. Evil acts committed by the aliens, villains, or agents of the anomaly can more easily be excused than those committed by the hero. The alterations and adaptations undergone by this agent of reality often require suspension of traditional ethical codes. And how many of these codes a hero can break before he has moved outside the implied limits of a formula (and a genre) became a frequent problem for 30s SF writers.

Lee Bentley, hero of Arthur Burks's story, "Manape the Mighty" (*AS,* June 1931), is shipwrecked with a beautiful woman on an island inhabited by Caleb Barter, a "mad" scientist. "Here," the narrator remarks of the situation, "barriers of convention were razed as simply and naturally as among children."[10] Acknowledging, even promising, that this setting will allow all variety of taboo-breaking, Burks (who, incidentally, was a highly successful and prolific pulp writer) goes on to place Bentley in situations which come perilously close to sullying this hero's status as agent of reality. Bentley's brain, for example, is transplanted into an ape's body, while his body receives the ape's brain. The presence of a very attractive woman complicates matters, and makes perverse any sort of sexual possibility. The mad scientist sums it up: "Your human cunning, hampered by your simian body, pitted against the highly specialized body of your former self, in turn hampered by the lack of reasoning of an ape—in a contest in a primitive surrounding for a female! A glorious experiment!" (p. 331). Since the hero is essentially split, and each half is combined with the complementary half of an ape, the possibility of sexual defilement is greatly magnified. Union between the woman (or the female apes) and either the man with the ape's brain or the ape with the man's brain seems equally grotesque. Ellen Estabrook, the in-génue, emphatically states the body of Lee Bentley "must never be permitted to do anything of which Lee Bentley of after years may have cause to feel ashamed" (p. 347)—blithely ignoring any pos-sibility that they will be killed. In "Manape the Mighty" Burks sets up a situation in which the anomaly—a biological change—pro-vides opportunities for the hero very nearly to overstep clear-cut moral parameters. And the skillful way the situation consciously recalls and challenges social strictures (here, bestiality and, by im-plication miscegenation) makes the story exciting despite its fairly predictable pattern and foregone conclusion, in which reality is ful-ly restored, and brains are returned to their original bodies.

Another artful tack the writer of the status quo SF story can take involves creating a tension between the attractiveness of the SF anomaly and the anomaly's potential for evil or destruc-tiveness. A writer can spark the reader's enthusiasm for and appreciation of an anomaly. It can seem like a perfectly good idea, a reasonable experiment, say, with intelligently planned and practical ends. Yet a small misgiving that might appear early on magnifies as the experiment and the story move toward their conclusions. Nat Schachner's "The 100th Generation" (*AS,* May 1934) follows such a pattern. It concerns the eugenic experiments of a millionaire scientist, Bayley Spears, and his friend Radburn Phelps (the narrator). Spears outlines his experiment: using the sperm and ova of famous people, he plans to produce a super race: "Within the space of one year, by continued fertilizations of mesoderm germ plasma, we shall have telescoped a hundred generations and skipped almost three thousand years of human life."[11] Initially, Phelps seems a little dazed and awed by this idea, but he helps carry out the experiment just the same. He becomes caught up in the millionaire's enthusiasm and earnestness—as indeed the reader is caught up, too. This seems a way to carry out eugenic experiments without the tyranny of selecting who should and who should not be allowed to reproduce, a way of bettering the race's genetic stock without the usual qualms con-cerning social disruption. And when Phelps finally does voice his objections, they seem after-the-fact, possibly even petty: he says the creatures will not have responded to environmental influences, and will be too inbred. He then distances himself from the experiment altogether, and lets Spear go to a remote island with the embryos.

The tension between the possibility of carrying out such an experiment—compressing three thousand years into twenty—and the experimental technique's unforeseen ramifications resolves itself when Spears sends Phelps a telegram requesting that the remote island be immediately blown up. The experiment apparently ended in failure. Schachner consciously creates an interesting tension: when Phelps lands on the island, the first creature he sees is a beautiful woman, seemingly an ideal result of eugenic experimentation. Why blow up the island? "Never in all my years had I seen such a glorious creature" (p. 93), Phelps thinks to himself. And the reader hopes that this woman (named "Una") will be representative. She proves, however, the exception to the rule, and the rest of the hundredth generation are so monstrous that they plan to vivisect the landing party. Fortunately this plan fails. Reality reestablishes itself in the form of a romance that springs up between Phelps's son and Una. Throughout, Schachner skillfully divides the reader's feeling between an enthusiasm for the experiment—reified fully in the person of Una—and fear of its terrifying failure.

The attractiveness-repulsiveness dichotomy in status quo SF formulas ultimately became so central that its writers shaped the status quo story into other versions of itself. Some stories show the anomaly as entirely positive, so much so that reality (flawed as it is) cannot accept it. This pattern I call the inverted status quo. Another version, the transplanted type status quo formula, begins with an anomalous situation (such as a space flight to Andromeda) into which an even more anomalous agent intrudes (a "black hole" in space, for example). As the anomaly becomes more and more attractive, the desire to expel it becomes weaker: instead of chronicling the machinations of expulsion, the later, more complex and more sophisticated status quo formulas question the necessity of such expulsion, and examine the underlying instincts and motivations for the reader's attraction to this anomalous element.

In the following section, I will analyze one story, "Origin of Thought," by Spencer Lane. This story (and the ones used in the following chapters) is meant to be exemplary, but represents neither the earliest nor perhaps the most influential enactment of a formula. SF authors did not consciously pattern their works after certain paradigmatic stories. Rather, they undoubtedly read and assimilated a great deal of the fiction that was printed, and strove to make their stories both somewhat imitative and somewhat distinctive. The stories I have chosen are perceived to be distillations of formulaic patterns, patterns that only occasionally appeared in such pure form. Although many other stories more or less fit formulaic patterns, and would decidedly fall into one category or another, they did not fulfill every feature of the stereotypical tale. Status quo stories, for example, in which the hero is sacrificed to save the world (and to assure the restoration of reality) did appear, but were not the standard fare. Each story used as an example will therefore be viewed as both a model of a given formula and as a departure from an entirely conventional ur-text.

It is not surprising that Spencer Lane—actually a "house pseudonym" for an author whose real identity will never be disclosed,[12] probably an editor or group of editors at *Astounding*—wrote a quintessentially formulaic status quo SF story, "Origin of Thought" (*ASF*, July 1938). The story opens with a fairly typical picture of thirties reality, moves into what seems a dangerous anomaly, and concludes with an expulsion, in fact an abandonment of the anomaly altogether. Much shorter than most stories in *Astounding*, "Origin of Thought" was probably intended to be used to fill a space in the magazine. The mid-thirties *Astounding* prided itself on having both the largest circulation of any SF pulp and the most pages—160—and no doubt kept a number of fairly conventional stories on hand that could be easily trimmed or padded to round out an issue. Because they did not have to please editors or stand out in any particular way, these stories often followed formulas more slavishly than author-written (as opposed to editor-written) fiction could ever have done. They bring together conventional features whose confluence would ordinarily make a story unsaleable, but which also renders it archetypal.

The "reality" with which "Origin of Thought" opens securely mirrors 30s America. It is a picture of a hungry man trying to find a job.

> Jerry Moore read the advertisement through once more and flung the paper down disgustedly. He hitched his hat lower over his eyes, fingered the last, lone nickel in his pocket,

then slowly reached down for the paper. The words "Good
Salary" stuck and danced before his eyes like a barber pole
on a spree.[13]

A little later, we learn that "Jerry hadn't had a square meal in
three days" (p. 101). Yet this hero has not been downtrodden
all his life. His father, apparently, had been a rich man, and
Jerry has never had to work before. "Jerry's lifelong experience
had been made up of spending the money his father had left
him" (p. 101). About Jerry's physical person little is disclosed:
enough possibility inheres in his great physical discomfort and
hunger, his awareness of personal failure, and his previous association with some wealth and social position. These qualities and
conditions mesh nicely with the common Depression picture of
a hungry, out-of-work man and a situation the reader can find
both familiar and slightly exotic. The traditional view of a downtrodden individual is mitigated by his former social station and a
decided pluckiness. He answers the advertisement.

The anomaly follows fairly conventional patterns. Jerry takes
a job (getting it because the employer, Professor Abelard Hill,
attended college with Jerry's father) as the subject of a psychological
experiment. Professor Hill has gained a reputation for his statements on the nature of thought; he perceives it as something which
can have "active power," and which can, if harnessed, even
transport things. Jerry Moore is hired as a subject of an experiment
to transport a human to a distant place. Jerry himself, as well
as those who are to exert the "action of combined thought" on
him, has to be trained for the experiment, has to think "prescribed
thoughts without effort" (p. 103). On the day of the experiment,
Jerry—in addition to the many other followers of Hill—thinks
these thoughts and is immediately transported to a bizarre world
of gray mist, similar, in fact, to the world of many other alternate
universes in SF:

The ground was uneven. It seemed to sink under his feet,
like sponge rubber. . . . It almost seemed as if it hurt him
when he stepped on the surface, as if—he laughed a short,
frightened laugh—as if he were walking on the convolutions
of his own brain! (p. 104).

An environmental change here, to be sure, but soon the story reveals a concomitant biological change in Jerry: in this alternate reality, he can have anything he wants from the real world if he thinks about it with intense, sustained concentration. He thinks of a meal, eats it, and satisfies his hunger; he thinks of and produces a bed and washstand; he thinks of Helen (the Professor's attractive receptionist), and she too appears, perplexed and frightened. One part of the anomaly in "Origin of Thought" consists of a mist world into which the hero has the power to transport things from the real world. If anything is unique or unusual about this anomaly, it is its relative harmlessness, its surface-level self-sufficiency. As much as anything, the mist world reflects the authors' failure to imagine any definite setting.

Helen Hartford's appearance in this anomalous, other-plane world at once creates a conflict and reestablishes a connection with the familiar world. The anomaly is apparently disruptive, because each item Jerry produces through imagining simultaneously vanishes from the real world. At this point in the story, Jerry Moore's situation and power take on new meaning. Where previously the conflicts concerned his survival and existence (there might have been questions about his being alive, for example, or of his ability to sustain himself in this alternate world), the conflict now centers on the extent to which he will use his power. He can have, in effect, anything he wants—food, a bed, a woman. After Helen has rested on his bed, Jerry describes the situation to her, and her frightened reaction is at once understandable and calculated to force the reader into sharing her fear. The moral conflicts raised by the story are those that concern extramarital sex (possibly even rape). The story questions the extent to which society's laws and mores should be upheld by an individual who has been physically removed from society altogether and who, therefore, need not abide by laws and mores.

Perhaps the urgency Helen feels is based partly on knowledge of what Jerry could do if he wanted. Near the conclusion, when Jerry returns to the real world, Professor Hill voices a possibility that was implied by Jerry's situation: "You could have destroyed the Earth, could have created new galaxies" (p. 105). This threat is never explicitly stated in the text, however. Nor is the idea of paradise directly alluded to: in his situation, Jerry could have virtually anything he wanted, and it is surprising that he fails to exploit its possibilities more than he does. The section wherein Jerry exercises his powers may have been trimmed. Its episodic structure could easily be extended as the magazine's physical limitations required.

The expulsion of the anomaly is accomplished in a deliberate way, and presented as the best solution to the situation. Jerry returns Helen to the real world, deflating any possibility of her entanglement with him. There she organizes Hill's students into a group which can, with their combined mental effort, recall Jerry. Organization and energy from a large group conspire to right things. Professor Hill has meanwhile changed his teachings in order to avoid a possible repetition of the accident: "Certain trends of thought were eliminated. There was no longer any effort to transfer objects. All efforts were spent in expansion of the mind within the fields of ordinary endeavor" (p. 106). This effort on several planes (literally and figuratively speaking) is not only effectual—Jerry returns—but ultimately useful as well: Hill's new "courses were proving of greater value than during the time of more radical work" (p. 106). And the professor reforms, too. He tells Jerry: "I went too far but it'll never happen again. . . . What you learned must be forgotten, for the good of humanity" (p. 109). The students who sent and recalled Jerry are not likely to use their sinister power anymore, either. Upon his return "they fled like scared rabbits" (p. 109). Even the furniture materialized by Jerry in the other plane returns to its proper place.

The pleasing resolution of the fates of individual characters reinforces the sense of a properly and ideally restored reality. Jerry and Helen are to marry. Professor Hill, on the other hand, receives what he deserves: after Jerry comes back, the public denounces him as a "faker who perpetuated the greatest hoax of all time" (p. 109). Hill, who earlier had been obliquely likened to Prometheus, now has to endure public condemnation. Jerry and Helen meanwhile have become close to the Professor—he evidently is a charismatic figure who first brought the couple together. It is fitting, finally, that all their fates should be intertwined. Hill feels compelled to retreat from the public eye and the couple need a place to honeymoon. The story ends with the three planning a trip to the mountains, a socially-sanctioned place of retreat for both newlyweds and reprobate professors.

"Origin of Thought" has less aesthetic value than many other status quo SF tales, simply because it so faithfully adheres to the formula. Authors achieved artistic success in this type of story by exaggerating or creatively diverging from one of the basic elements. Reality is challenged so strongly that it very nearly collapses, in some offbeat, bizarre fashion, or certain situations elaborately challenge social/sexual taboos, or the anomaly presented is simultaneously attractive and threatening. This house-written "Spencer Lane" story could certainly have exploited such tensions more effectively were the middle section—that detailing the anomaly/reality conflict—simply longer. Jerry Moore does, after all, have an awesome power. Almost as an afterthought, it is pointed out that he could have used it for evil. The situation with Helen's visit (or summoning) could have been made more striking if her virtue had been more explicitly challenged. Similarly, the anomaly could have been shown to be both more attractive and more threatening; Jerry could have been shown enjoying his power more, and as being consciously aware that what he did had an effect on earth and the real world. These conflicts were all underdeveloped; Jerry was no sooner in the anomalous situation than he was out of it and safe. Concerns for his safety and curiosity about the exact circumstances of his dislocation overshadow the aforementioned, more provocative conflicts. Such conflicts are sacrificed to the constraints of pulp publishing, though. Functioning as it did in the magazine, as a filler, no doubt determined the story's length, and did not permit more than a relatively bland enactment of the formula.

"Origin of Thought," rather than actually speculating in any serious way about where people would go if they were "willed" far away (an absurd thought, anyway), or about the unlimited powers and potential of the human mind, shows a fairly quotidian social process: enculturation. Jerry Moore, a person who had never done anything but "spend the money his father had left him," is forced by circumstances to take a job, join the work force, study, go through a certain amount of traumatic experience, and finally win the admiration (and presumably love) of a woman. This process of enculturation shows Jerry a number of things about the way society operates, but perhaps the most striking personal revelation is that his individual consciousness counts for something and can have an effect on the world at large. The suggestion from the story's opening is that the main character has always been someone who had—or was forced—to define himself through his father and his father's wealth. But he discovers he can do things on his own, that he has a separate and even unique talent. It is significant that when Helen Hartford is summoned into Jerry's other-dimensional world, his ability to make "everything he saw in his mind" exist is not universal. Clearly this is not a talent everyone has. That Jerry employs it in a prudent, careful way suggests that he has accepted certain social responsibilities, too. His movement, from extreme penury through employment and study, to discovery of hidden personal resources and, finally, to marriage, is hardly an unusual one in fiction, nor is it a process that appears only in stories of science fiction.

But what keeps this story (and others like it) from being considered a fantasy entirely disconnected from any social reality is its aura of scientific plausibility. Though the actual experiment the story depicts seems patently ridiculous, the circumstances surrounding it are not. Abelard Hill, a professor, has his exploits and discoveries closely followed by the press. His methods can be taught; though they require hard, concentrated study, large numbers of people seem to be able to assimilate them just the same. Black Magic and witchcraft are not, that is, the operating principles. All the accoutrements of plausibility are present in "Origin of Thought." Even the experiment itself might not have seemed so far-fetched to readers of *Astounding,* who two years before (April-November, 1934) enjoyed an eight-part reprint serialization of Charles Fort's *Lo!* (1931), a tract in which paranormal phenomena are described and documented in great detail. Not only did Fort's work make for controversy in *Astounding*'s letters column, but it also served to bolster plausibility in SF stories. Publishing Fort's work was a deliberate ploy on the part of the editors to extend the realms of the possible far enough so that most of the stories they printed would fall within them. Once the plausibility of "Origin of Thought" is accepted, or at least once disbelief is suspended, the truth of the social process surrounding the story follows close behind. By removing the events of the story from a specific worldly setting and embedding in them a cluster of verification devices, authors were able to make a story's message more serious and weighty. The story catapults into the realm of a hypothetical or "test" situation which is freed from the necessity of adhering to standards set by non-SF. The hackneyed and banal are rendered important when clothed in scientific garb.

Why did such a variety of fiction emerge in large quantity from the thirties? Status quo SF, which usually affirms very conventional values, is in a way completely appropriate to the Depression era, during which such values were no doubt being questioned. "Origin of Thought" resembles many other stories in that such values as pertinacity, courage, steadfastness, loyalty, and love are cast in a positive light; pursuance of such values in fact ends up saving the world from destruction and saving Jerry Moore from personal disaster. Yet by using a science fictional story type, in which the reader's attention is displaced from the naturalistic, such values can be faced with impunity. They are operative, indeed, on an implicit level because, were they not so cast, they would be rejected as precisely the kinds of values that seemed no longer to be of any importance, whose applicability to modern life had been as much as usurped by the large-scale social and economic collapse of the thirties. The social process recollected by the standard status quo formula is often one that shows society's strength, adaptiveness, and ultimate integrity. That it has to accomplish this affirmation via dislocation and estrangement of course questions the very values it seeks to affirm but also suggests that the reading public was willing to be persuaded (even if subliminally) and reassured by them.

There are, additionally, certain fears this type of story expresses: for the social affirmation to work, the conflict society undergoes must have some genuine basis. The major fear this type of story plays on—and it can be connected to the 30s culture that nurtured it—is that society and all its conventional values will be unable to adapt to changed circumstances. The anomaly impinges upon reality in such a way that, for example, taboos are nearly broken and standard values discredited. In many stories, the conflict tests the central reality agents' ability to maintain probity when placed under the stress of unprecedented circumstances. And the reader undergoes a test when an anomaly appears simultaneously attractive and dangerous. Taboos and moral codes are only agreed upon in a society because the proscription of certain activities (murder, incest, and the like) is necessary for the society's self-preservation. The status quo SF story summons up fears of the loss of such self-protective behavior; though these stories end with reassurance, their primary narrative conflicts hinge on testing how far society and social values can be placed under the pressure of a distorting, outside influence and still be able to snap back to their original form. And finally this original form ends up being bolstered and validated.

The features of the late nineteenth and early twentieth centuries which produced such a formula (and even nurtured it) can be generalized about in a variety of ways. A narrative fictive structure that so strongly calls for and offers reassurance about existent social structures resembles in a way the actual reality of the times. From 1890 to 1930, the world had known a number of crises—a devastating world war, a huge population explosion, and the start of an economic depression; and several major technological advancements: the automobile, the airplane, widespread electrical power. It was a world that had been virtually remade in those forty years. Any close psychosocial connection between these crises and advancements and a new, highly popular form of literature must be conjectural and tentative. But the general pattern seems fairly clear: there was need for a type of fiction that mollified fears about the loss of values, stability, and security in the face of widespread, nearly overwhelming change. The status quo formula, with its insistence upon society's ability to recoup its losses, to recover its original form despite the intervention of alien—and even at times dangerously attractive—elements, filled this need. This narrative structure implies a reactionary kind of politics, one that suggests a return to past known quantities, a preservation of pre-World War I purity. Though this formula admits the possibility for change, and even the excitement inherent in facing it, the primary and overriding depiction of that change is as evil, something that should be ousted, and the mechanism for such expulsion works through traditional values.

THE TRANSPLANTED STATUS QUO TALE

The simple status quo tale was soon embellished by writers. They removed any directly representational form of social reality.

The section of "reality-anomaly conflict," the most elaborated and interesting section of the simple status quo SF formula, describes the entire narrative in the "transplanted status quo" variety; but the general movement of both varieties is similar. Basically, the transplanted status quo story opens in an anomalous circumstance—on a spaceship, on another planet, or at the earth's core. Into this "base level anomaly," complete with a cast of stereotypical characters, another far more "alien" anomaly intervenes. And this second anomaly forms the focus of the action and excitement in the transplanted status quo tale; as the conflict within it develops, the surrounding base level anomaly recedes, functioning much as "reality" functioned in the simple status quo tale.

The notorious "space opera" stories of the thirties and forties very closely follow this formula. Science fiction critics have long ridiculed such tales of adventure and intrigue in space, mostly on grounds that there is little need for the action to take place in space at all. The stories consist merely of heroes and villains, cops and robbers, or cowboys and Indians, at a very superficial and childish remove. The space setting seems only a clanking, technological backdrop, they argue, for old-fashioned "shootouts and action." To a certain extent, such criticisms are valid. Yet the structure itself should not be equated with its worst and most adolescent enactments. It proved a durable and—to the readers of other popular fiction, particularly westerns—a readily identifiable pattern in thirties SF. Most importantly, it developed its own conventions, which eventually separated it from other "adventure" forms.

The transplanted status quo tale usually opens with a picture of the transplanted reality. The opening phase of the story is either characterized by restiveness—the crew is anxious to dock, say, or to find excitement—or by a prevailing indolence similar to that found in the opening of the simple status quo tale. In both instances a sense of something about to happen pervades the opening sequences. Often a slightly distracting minor incident whets the reader's appetite for excitement. A power failure almost occurs on board the spaceship, or one of the crew members falls ill.

An alternative pattern starts with the depiction of the anomaly or alien that the transplanted reality will no doubt encounter, but it, too, is in either a passive or a dormant state. A. E. Van Vogt's

opening line to "Black Destroyer" (*ASF*, July 1939) is an excellent
example of alien dormancy: "On and on Coeurl prowled!"[14]
This is a state from which adventure will be generated, an opening
that promises action and conflict. The conflict usually comes
gradually rather than all at once. The anomaly is either encountered
by the agents of a near-recognizable reality, or these familiar
types actively seek out the anomaly. Coeurl is met by a spaceship
of men; Northwest Smith encounters a "Shambleau" in C. L.
Moore's story of the same title (*Weird Tales,* 1933). These encounters are not initially frightening, not really anything too far
removed from routine. Coeurl is perhaps a little frightful at first
to the men, but they fit it into categories:

> "I'd hate to meet that baby on a dark night in an alley."
> "Don't be silly. This is obviously an intelligent creature.
> Probably a member of the ruling race."
> "It looks like nothing else than a big cat, if you forget
> those tentacles sticking out from its shoulders, and making
> allowances for those monster forelegs."
> "Its physical development . . . presupposes an animal-like
> adaptation to its surroundings, not an intellectual one."

The Shambleau Northwest Smith comes upon is being lynched,
and Smith rescues it from this fate. The initial meeting is a slight
shock, but, like the meeting with Coeurl, it is padded by the
transplantation of reality. The reader is able to suspend his fear
that this encounter is potentially dangerous—things like this
happen in space all the time—and is asked to share the values
of the reality agent.

Science fiction writers frequently exploit the reader's uncertainty
as to how much of the circumstance is a function of, say, the
usual hardships or peculiarities of space flight, and how much is
to be considered alarming.

The anomaly itself is usually some kind of alien life form whose
destructiveness and evil are gradually revealed to the crew (and
to the reader) as the story unfolds. Occasionally, the life form is
not overtly vile, but insidiously evil. Such a situation prolongs
the reader's tension over what portion of the anomalous situation
is usual and what is threatening. Yet this variation does not really
change the pattern of action. As the story moves to a climax,

and the true nature of the anomaly is revealed, the interaction between it and the reality agents degenerates into some fairly conventional action sequence—fight, chase, showdown, and the like: most SF stories generally have more intriguing openings than endings.

In the better transplanted status quo tale, the imagery used throughout this conflict usually suggests some easily identifiable earth-bound concern—hunger, sexuality, or work, for example—and it is finally that image pattern that suggests the meaning of the story. The Coeurl's hunger in "Black Destroyer" reveals it to be a primitive creature unable to comprehend the vast organizational strength of the men it encounters. This lack of comprehension, this primitive drive, causes the Coeurl's destruction despite its enormous physical powers. The Shambleau's unfettered sexuality entwines Northwest Smith in a way that suggests such sensuality is evil, destructive.

This encounter between an embodiment of some real world concern and a transplanted reality makes an oblique—but often effective—comment on surrounding naturalistic reality. At the story's end order is restored, the alien or evil anomaly is thrust out, and the transplanted reality survives. Usually the story takes the encounter as a warning (as the reader might take it as a warning about him or herself or society) but generally the statement is a conservative one: old values are upheld, the single facet of reality that the anomaly epitomized is put in its proper place, and the crew or reality agent is left to find other, new, exciting adventures. The *Enterprise* of "Star Trek" continues to "explore new worlds, to seek out new life and new civilizations, to boldly go where no man has gone before"[15]—week after week.

It is not surprising that science fiction appropriated this structure, which has so many similarities to other popular forms of fiction. One main similarity is that the action and characters are isolated throughout from the rest of civilization. Such a feature is apparent in sea stories, air stories, Gothic tales (especially those set in castles), and many detective stories. Its effect is that of providing a counterreality that acts as a microcosm in which natural, everyday laws have only a limited applicability. This isolation, which must of course take place to an extent in all fiction, becomes almost hermetic in the transplanted SF tale.

The popular form closest to the transplanted SF tale is the

western. The western is set in a locale which is not only isolated from civilization, but which works by its own set of rules, and a western story's resolution must, like that offered by a transplanted SF tale, be effected in this setting, through these laws. Much space is devoted in both types of story to establishing this setting as a counterreality, filling it with enough detail and local color so that it takes on not so much a believability as an identifiable character. In SF, this is the milieu into which the transplanted reality must convincingly fit; the more replete this milieu is with its own unique features and the more striking the contrast between it and the agents of reality, the more the latter will have to accede to its laws and codes. Many of the details can be brought out in the confrontation between the transplanted reality and the anomaly, but in this form of SF the milieu itself, like that in the western story, permeates the tale to such an extent that it becomes almost a character in its own right.

The use of local color suggests nostalgia for simpler times and simpler conflicts than could be found in more realistic fiction; in science fiction it serves to reduce the complexities of the unknown into comprehensible patterns. Stanley G. Weinbaum, a master of local color in the transplanted status quo tale, describes a meeting between "Ham" Hammond and a Venusian in "Parasite Planet" (*AS*. February 1935):

> . . . Ham stopped for a palaver.
> "*Murra*," he said.
> The language of the natives of the equatorial regions of the Hotlands is a queer one. It has, perhaps, two hundred words, but when a trader had learned those two hundred, his knowledge of the tongue is but little greater than the man who knows none at all.
> The words are generalized, and each sound has anywhere from a dozen to a hundred meanings. *Murra,* for instance, is a word of greeting; it may mean something much like "hello," or "good morning." It may also convey a challenge—"on guard!" It means besides "Let's be friends," and also, strangely, "Let's fight this out."[16]

Certainly it is difficult to communicate with the natives of Venus, but by immersing oneself in a culture, and adopting a nonthreatening stance, one can negotiate even the most ambiguous aspects of language. This meeting, which necessitates the reduction of language, the categorizing of words, and the like, resembles more than anything else the encounter between a cowpoke and an Indian, each suspicious of the other but able to communicate their straightforward ideas just the same. After a short discourse on the difficulty English must pose to non-native speakers, the passage continues:

> But this one accepted the intended sense. *"Murra,"* he responded, pausing. *"Usk?"* That was among other things, "Who are You?" or "Where did you come from?" or "Where are you bound?"
>
> Ham chose the latter sense. He pointed off into the dim west, then raised his hand in an arc to indicate the mountains. *"Erotia,"* he said. That had but one meaning, at least.

This is a planet peopled with four-legged, three-eyed creatures, their language and ways resembling those of the primitive. More importantly, the landscape to the west has mountains whither explorers go. Though the real west is a thing of the past, a frontier yet exists on other worlds.

As the above quotation suggests, another aspect of the western borrowed by the transplanted status quo SF tale is the creation of a setting in which Anglo-Saxons can triumph over both dangerous natives and a dangerous environment. It is the wise, worldly "Ham" who reverts to the simple native dialect, who runs through the multiple meanings of native words in his mind, who is the representative of the highly adaptive life form in a foreign land-scape. Though Weinbaum's story does not seem to suggest specific real-world analogues, many stories of the thirties clearly do. Anthony Gilmore's "Hawk" Carse stories, published in the early thirties in *Astounding*, pit the Anglo Hawk against the decidedly Oriental villain, Ku Sui. They fight each other in landscapes that look quite familiar (a corral, for example), and they wear their ray guns low on their hips.[17]

A further feature of the western that this variety of SF was able to exploit is the emergence of a hero. Though a hero usually comes out of the simple status quo story, the focus is usually on

a struggle for survival that itself makes and chooses heroes. Sometimes, in the simple status quo tale, the hero is a composite being
(quite literally) created by a society which knows that it is struggling
for its very existence.[18] The situation in the transplanted tale,
however, is one that involves recurrent risk-taking: heroism is a
way of life for the space captain, much as it is for the cowboy
protagonist. Hawk Carse did the most, we are told, to "shape the
raw frontiers of space," and is known as "he of the spitting
ray gun and the phenomenal draw." Northwest Smith, C. L.
Moore's creation, also seems transplanted from a western:

> Tall Earthman in the space explorer's leathern garb, all one
> color from the burning of savage suns save for the sinister
> pallor of his no-colored eyes in a seamed and resolute face . . .
> [he was] lounging negligently against the wall, arms folded
> and gun-hand draped over his left forearm . . . [he] looked
> incapable of swift motion.[19]

Owen Wister's description of the "Virginian" is remarkably
similar. Both men share a dusty, rugged physical appearance; both
have a languid bearing.

> Lounging there at ease against the wall was a slim young
> giant, more beautiful than pictures. His broad, soft hat was
> pushed back. A loose-knotted, dull scarlet handkerchief
> sagged from his throat, and one casual thumb was hooked
> in the cartridge belt that slanted across his hips. He had
> plainly come many miles from somewhere across the vast
> horizon, as the dust upon him showed. His boots were white
> with it. His overalls were gray with it.[20]

These are the types who—in two major forms of popular fiction—
epitomize and fight for honest, American values in dangerous
frontiers.

Because two main features of the transplanted status quo tale
were the alien landscape and the hero, this formula lent itself to
serialization and therefore found much currency among early SF
pulp writers. The evil circumstances of the alien landscape could
change, but the agent of reality (and often the primary agent of

evil, such as Ku Sui) remained the same, and essentially maintained on ongoing strife. The "hero" pulps (*Doc Savage, G-8, The
Shadow, The Avenger*), however, capitalized on this narrative
situation more successfully than the SF writers, and the later
thirties SF magazines did not stress the hero.[21] The SF sequels
would run four, or sometimes six, stories in length and would
soon be replaced by stories with similar, but slightly changed
heroes. The SF pulps were more interested in extraordinary
circumstances than superhuman heroes.[22]

Though there are many similarities between the transplanted
status quo story and the western, the former was easily able to
distinguish itself from the latter. Science fiction's subject—some
kind of anomaly or change—was what redeemed it from being a
routine embellishment of westerns or Gothics. Although the plausibility of such science fiction stories is minimal, the scientific
terms used in the stories project an air of authenticity, remove the
tale from a strictly romantic mode, and finally allow it to address
a major relationship in contemporary American society: that
between man and technology.

The initial transplantation of quotidian reality into a spaceship
or even into a future, highly advanced, postindustrial world
immediately implies an interpretation of those technological
surroundings. Often, of course, the surroundings recede into
relative unimportance: the adventure, or the encounter with the
alien, or the war, is stressed. But just as often, the technology
present in the transplantation of reality is all that stands between
the group of heroes—agents of a known, identifiable culture—and
the generally destructive or strange forces they encounter. The
action demonstrates what sorts of things technology is to be relied
upon to produce. Often the evil or alien forces that the reality
agents encounter will be using a similar technology in an entirely
contrary way.

"Seeker of To-Morrow" (*AS*, July 1937), by Eric Frank Russell
and Leslie T. Johnson, is the story of time traveler Glyn Weston,
who progresses into the future, stopping at various places in
man's history to discover what life is like. Eventually, he goes too
far into the future and dies because there is not any air left. He is
fortunately rescued and revived by Venusians. They have migrated
from earth. Between the time of Weston's arrival on Venus and

his departure in 1998, earth's societies have degenerated because they have misused technology (mainly guns and weapons). In the world of Venus in the far off future, there are a number of beneficial technological changes—the "normality chamber" in which Weston is resuscitated, "stereo-vision," apparently a version of television, even an "automatic back-scratcher." This technology stands in marked contrast to that of A.D. 2486, when "warfare has now reached the stage of perfection where nobody wins and everybody loses."[23] The authors use the time travel structure to showcase various technological developments including moving roads, synthetic clothing, and robot travel. Though its authors do not link one specific social organization to one use of technology, "Seeker of To-Morrow" is an inventive use of the transplanted status quo formula which deviates considerably from its popular literary roots. And its emphasis on new technologies is one that this still emerging type of fiction could claim as its own.

"HOTEL COSMOS": A TRANSPLANTED STATUS QUO STORY

Raymond Z. Gallun's "Hotel Cosmos" (*ASF*, July 1938) typifies the transplanted status quo structure. A story about a future hotel that houses alien beings who are unable to exist in earth's atmosphere, it manages to combine the tropes and conventions of a number of popular forms—Gothic, adventure, detective, and western—but still maintains an aura of plausibility that the SF terms bring with them. The story lends itself well to discussion in terms of its structural characteristics, and finally demonstrates why the transplanted status quo structure eventually came to be used only for the most juvenile science fiction, and was replaced by other more sophisticated, more literary formulas.

The premise of "Hotel Cosmos" is that aliens, while residing on earth, can only stay in a hotel that has specially sealed and prepared rooms—ones that simulate their native environment as closely as possible. The story centers, however, on Dave Ledrack, the caretaker of this hotel. He attempts to find the slayer of various delegates and ambassadors from other worlds who are lodging in the hotel. Dave, not wanting to upset the precarious balance of intergalactic power, has to keep the "galactic celebrities" calm, and convince them that earth is not responsible for the deaths and disorder. As the story draws to a conclusion, it is evident that one of the aliens in the hotel has constructed some sophisticated mechanism that can make all life forms turn hostile and aggressive. Dave uncovers and kills this villain.

One major popular genre this story suggests is the Gothic tale. The hotel is similar to a castle. It is, like a castle, isolated, and the problem there is at first mysterious, even supernatural-sounding. But most important, the actual decor resembles that found in a Gothic novel. The hotel houses unknown things that creep and crawl and who are brought in in boxes resembling coffins. And initially there is a suggestion of opulence reminiscent of castles.

> The aspect of all the corridors of the building was much the same. Their floors were heavily carpeted; the walls, of tooled metal, were dully shining in the subdued green glow of the lights. Their uniformity was broken at regular intervals by airtight circular doors, which resembled in a somewhat less massive form the portals of bank vaults. Each door displayed a number, wrought in black onyx inlay, and mounted on each were several small valve wheels for regulating and adjusting the temperature, pressure, and gaseous composition of the atmosphere of the room within. The twilight was eerie and soft, and the sweeping sameness of the halls suggested the interminable distances seen in opposed mirrors.[24]

Behind some of these portals strange things are going on; it is up to our hero to find out what sorts of things these are. The Gothic setting provides the necessary enclosure that castles give in such tales, but also imparts a mystery that heightens tension, and suggests to the reader that rational laws may not be operative.

What goes on in this setting of technological mystery is, quite expectedly, action and adventure. *Astounding Stories,* which had started as essentially an action and adventure magazine, still relied heavily on such elements as the thirties drew to a close. There are, in "Hotel Cosmos," blaster weapons, ether phones, struggles with "proxy robots," and characters "furious with rage," not to mention the usual fights in hallways, broken orders, and last-minute reprieves. In short, the story has all the accoutrements of the "space opera" that critics have almost unanimously cited as childish and immature. But in this tale these elements are carefully calculated to mesh with other levels of popular literature conventions: the SF action holds together all the disparate popular genre elements.

The pattern of action is shaped, too, by the science fictional premise. Once the setting is displayed, it is virtually forgotten: the kinds of conflicts such a setting could stimulate are left to the reader's imagination. Surrounded by hundreds of aliens living in small enclaves of safety, Dave Ledrack could have any number of adventures involving confusion with atmosphere controls, or sundry troubles could arise from the necessary life-support systems. It is a setting that implies a great deal of action in the everyday life of Dave Ledrack, but it is not that action the story finally delivers. In a story from the early thirties, contrarily, some of this daily action might have been dramatized; here, in the late thirties, with *ASF* under Campbell's editorship, such pulp padding was less common. Indeed, Gallun goes striaght to the nub of the conflict, and brings the second-level anomaly into the story quite early on. He lets the reader—whose intelligence and experience with SF are assumed—flesh out the world Dave Ledrack lives in.

Dave must find out which of the delegates has been committing the murders, and this involves deciding which of them is the most likely suspect. The detection does seem a little primitive. The only clues are that the murders are being committed by proxy robots (that is, robots controlled by aliens who themselves cannot leave their sealed chambers), and the hotel staff itself seems to be gripped with a kind of "murder madness." Dave locates the prime suspect, named 4-2-5, and catches him in the act of using some superscientific device that has the effect of making living creatures lust to kill. The detection could have been more elaborate, but it does share certain elements with the detective story: a detective who does not want outside interference, a very limited set of clues to a crime that could have far-reaching consequences, and finally, an explanation that leaves a small element of mystery but explains all the major features of the crime.[25]

Curiously, though, the hero in this tale does not really resemble the standard detective hero: Dave Ledrack seems to have been lifted instead from a western story. His nickname is "easy-goin' "—one certainly more suited to the temperament of the western hero than to the more ratiocinative ones of detective heroes like Auguste Dupin, Sherlock Holmes, or even the active and importunate Sam Spade. It is Dave's easy-going nature that allows him to resist the attack of 4-2-5: "he was one man in a million as far as emotional makeup went" (p. 150). Like the lounging, carefree cowboy, Ledrack draws his strength from his "cool" temperament; his ability to handle himself in difficult situations is much like the western hero's poise under fire.

"Hotel Cosmos," like other stories of its variety, represents an immature stage of the genre, in which SF writers were attempting to find an idiom and structure amid tropes and conventions of many other popular forms. Though imaginative and well-written, the story struggles against the limitations of its formula. A version of reality as it existed at the story's opening had to be restored by its conclusion, even though it is clear Gallun was far more interested in the slimy monstrosities of other planets than he was in the plight of Dave Ledrack, who was maintaining them in a hotel on earth. Later SF explores such "alien" problems, and forgets altogether about the ascendancy of a version of status quo reality.

Indeed, the transplanted status quo SF story eventually evolved into the story of the alternative world, in which the focus was not so much earth values, or earth-like personalities, but on the very strange. The transplanted story is evidence of how SF writers were attempting to transcend their popular culture antecedents and find their own set of conventions and situation, ones that were not entirely analogous to those found in other forms. Writers did this in an indirect way that perhaps did result in selecting the most important SF elements: by employing many conventions of other genres, the SF-specific elements stood out and were often cited by readers as ones they wanted to see repeated—at the expense of elements that they saw so frequently in other pulp magazines. It was the winnowing-out of this status quo variety from the major SF magazines that finally suggested that some elements found in other pulp formats—the Gothic setting, the western hero, and detection—were not, heaped together, what serious readers thought of as science fiction.

THE INVERTED STATUS QUO STORY

It is not surprising that the simple status quo story became quickly outmoded; SF authors realized that to keep the genre alive, they had to play off rather than religiously adhere to the basic formula. One spin-off is a type of SF tale that, while grounded in and framed by a picture of familiar reality, shows a positive or useful anomaly that is thrust out in much the same way as is the anomaly in the basic form. The status quo is depicted in an unflattering light, while the encroaching anomaly is made to appear attractive. This structure shows an inversion of the attitudes displayed toward reality and anomaly in the standard status quo tale. Though not a very large number of such tales appeared in the thirties, this formula—the inverted status quo—is a significant offshoot of the standard type, which ends up depicting the organization of society in ways diametrically different from the affirmative, reassuring ones of the standard form. And this emergence of a kind of SF which could at once work within the status quo formula and question the values the structure itself seems to imply, opens the way for emergence of new formulas altogether, ones that do not rely so heavily on a picture of reality and a bolstering of the status quo.

The positive anomaly introduced into this reality is, often, of a technological nature, the "better mousetrap" sprung instantly into a world or situation not quite ready for it. Donald Wandrei's "Murray's Light" (*AS*, June 1935), for example, centers on D. V. Murray and his invention, the "Arctolight." This is a lamp that provides a "soft, steady, strong light that fills the room with an even and restful illunination,"[26] requires no electricity or outside power, and lasts "six months, perhaps, indefinitely" (p. 36). Another sort of positive-value anomaly is presented in "Manna from Mars" (*AS*, March 1934) by Stanton A. Coblentz, in which a "radio amplifying plan of interplanetary communication"[27] leads to Mars sending earth an ideal food, the "sugar-leaf": "food which is really fruit, bread, and meat all in one" (p. 48), and can be cultivated virtually anywhere. Other varieties of the unprecedented but apparently wonderful SF element in this type of story include cures for diseases, serums that will provide eternal youth or extreme adaptiveness, and machines that help uncover vast bodies of knowledge.

One major tension in the inverted status quo is between the utility of scientific breakthroughs and their lasting, trouble-free function. What might, for example, appear to be very useful or exciting, perhaps even life-saving, may prove to have either a very short useful life or unpleasant side effects. Though this transformation of the SF element from a positive one into a potentially threatening one would seem to suggest no difference between these stories and those in the standard status quo formula, the reality-anomaly interplay differs significantly. Society's use of the breakthrough causes the problem, not the discovery itself. Nat Schachner's story, "The Ultimate Metal" (AS, February 1935), concerns the discovery of "Coultonite," a substance that is extremely strong and also provides light: "It never faded; it never succumbed to the ordinary annoyances of burned out fuels, defective bulbs, overloaded lines; it shed its eye-resting illumination into every nook and cranny of every office, and the dull silvery metal lent itself to rich and tasteful decorative effects."[28] A building made of this substance collapses, though, as the element apparently lasts only a short time in a stable form. The invention or discovery itself is clearly not at fault in the story; it is the rich sponsor of the research—as well as the society so structured that research cannot go on without rich, meddlesome sponsors—who is to blame. Thomas Coulton immediately seeks to make a monument of Coultonite (whose discovery he has taken the credit for) and stubbornly refuses to have the disintegrating building vacated: both decisions are scientifically unsound because they are made by a pseudoscientist. The cause of the disaster may therefore be traced to flaws in character or society. As in many SF stories of this type, the anomaly is used merely as a device by which the author can offer a criticism of one complex of social processes. Being scientifically grounded, the anomaly serves as a means to make the story topical, and the scientific explanation keeps it in the realm of the possible, real world. The anomaly is fiction, too. Coultonite and the inventor and the building itself do not exist. They are sufficiently removed from reality so that the average reader will not be prepared to contrast his opinion on the matter with the author's version. That Coultonite's remarkable properties do not last is in no way an issue the reader can take a stance on: he simply must accept the social corruption Schachner posits as the agent responsible for the building's collapse. The impression is that if society were more perfect in the ways it implements change, this marvelous invention could have been used beneficially instead of ending up as a disaster.

The tension between a miracle drug's potential for good and its harmful side effects is similarly resolved in this type of story: some flawed social process is at fault, and turns sour the hope such a drug might bring. In Stanley G. Weinbaum's "The Adaptive Ultimate" (*AS*, November 1935), for example, the *drosophila*-based serum used to cure a working-class woman's tuberculosis is successful against the disease but creates a near superhuman who uses her newly acquired powers to compensate for the pains she suffered as a shop girl. "Would you have me resume the life that sent me into your hands?" she asks her bewildered doctor after she has been cured and displays criminal tendencies.[29] After being acquitted for a murder she has committed, she seeks political power. The impression is that if she wanted power at any time after the treatment she could have taken it. Despite these "side effects," the nature of the serum—its ability to turn a "drab, ugly, uneducated girl" (p. 111) into a beautiful, effectual, and poised woman—is marvelous. The doctor's plans for her after she has healed ("she could help the housekeeper" [p. 111]) seem almost as bad as the destructiveness her cure/transformation brings. The suggestion Weinbaum seems to be making is that if there were fewer distinctions (specifically in terms of wealth and social station) among people, such a serum might be useful indeed; a race of superhumans could prosper if the vindictiveness and enmity that come with social oppression did not exist.

The volatility of international relations is also frequently emphasized in the inverted status quo story. The tension between the attractiveness of the anomaly and the world's inability to accept it makes this formula an interesting alternative to the usual status quo variety. Stanton A. Coblentz's "Manna from Mars" epitomizes this type of story; the Martians send éarth seeds for an ideal food—the "sugar-leaf"—but they fail to land it in the agreed-upon location, and a huge global war ensues. The anomaly—a type of plant that will solve immediately and for perpetuity the problem of hunger—is certainly a positive one, but international political strife makes such a change impossible despite its overwhelming usefulness. Many of Coblentz's stories make a similar pessimistic statement, as do some more contemporary SF stories: reality as we know it, they say, is simply not ready for major changes of any kind. The possibility is mentioned in "Manna" that the whole debacle was caused by a hoax; but that issue, finally, is somewhat beside the point: the international balance of power is shaky and tenuous whether the sugar-leaf exists or not.

The weakness not so much of the social structure but of human nature itself creates tension in many inverted status quo stories. When people find out too much about themselves or their characters, they become terrified and sociopathic in some stories of this type. These tales exploit the tension between the desire to find out hidden or arcane knowledge and the desire to suppress this often important information. In A. T. Locke's "The Machine That Knew Too Much" (AS, December 1933) a machine has been invented that can reproduce any sound ever made: "Deeds, words and even thoughts—all are indelibly recorded somewhere among the great and mysterious forces of the universe, and some day the record will be revealed to all who care to read."[30] Such an invention is indeed marvelous, and could be extremely useful, but it could also encourage a kind of paranoia: "*Even now*," the story's closing words declare, "*there is a Thing that is listening, listening, listening*"(p. 39). What is finally revealed is that Forsythe, the protagonist, has murdered a friend to get the machine, and he often listens to it replay the murder. When he is discovered at this obsessive habit, he kills himself. Such a machine, the story suggests, would create more problems than it could ever solve. Coblentz's "The Truth About the Psycho-Tector" (AS, October 1934) raises a similar issue. The psycho-tector is meant to "analyze the hidden bents and potentialities of the human mind."[31] Not surprisingly, it causes a great deal of turmoil, for it "had no tact; it never hesitated to tell the unblushing truth" (p. 89). People accuse the machine of being a fraud, and its inventor, Alexander J. Shotgrass, is arrested. On trial, he has the machine tell the judge and jury not the truth, but what they want to hear about themselves, and he is acquitted. Like the invention in "The Machine That Knew Too Much," the psycho-tector offers an enormous body of knowledge to society, but the knowledge is forbidden. Both stories suggest that there are limits beyond which knowledge cannot comfortably extend, and that the final reassertion of norms, flawed as they are, may be inevitable; ignorance may be necessary to the preservation of social integrity.

Perhaps the most exciting conflict in the inverted status quo tale is that found in the atomic power story between the extraordinary usefulness of such power and the ability of man to use it in an appropriate fashion: even before atomic power existed *per se,* science fiction stories addressed this issue. Charles Willard Diffin's "The Power and the Glory" (*AS,* July 1930) discusses "the disintegration of the atom and the release of power unlimited."[32] Professor Eddinger cautions his star student, Avery, about the use of such power. " 'The law of compensation,' said Professor Eddinger. 'Two sides to the medal! Darkness and light—good and evil—life . . . and death!' " (p. 107). While Diffin is concerned with the potential physical destructiveness of such power, John W. Campbell, in "Elimination" (*AS,* May 1936), depicts the shelving of an enormous power resource because "it would destroy our greatest resource, the financial structure of the nation."[33] Campbell's story uses the example of an enormous power resource to philosophize about change: "There must be, you are saying, no real improvements, only little gadgets. There must be no Faradays who discover principles, only Sam Browns who invent new can openers and better mousetraps" (p. 46). An idea that Campbell voices in editorials for *Astounding,* this concept of gradual change describes adequately the social theory implied by the inverted status quo tale. The rejection of the anomaly—positive though it may potentially be—is not so much a demonstration of society's inherent weakness as a representation of the necessity of gradual change.

Inasmuch as the inverted status quo pattern is itself a derivative of the status quo formula, its aesthetic value is somewhat easier to assess. It raises expectations, for example, that are dispelled in an artful way as the author fails to adhere to the formula he appears to be working in. The pattern the inverted status quo most closely resembles—that is, the type of SF story that works through creating a tension between the anomaly's capacity for good and its potential for evil—is the one immediately invoked by most inverted status quo tales. These stories open with a familiar picture of reality, and then move into a representation of what seems to be a highly useful and positive anomaly, one that will help society. In the status quo tale, this anomaly will prove dangerous and even threatening to society, while in the inverted formula, it will prove to be much as it initially appeared, that is, beneficial to mankind—perhaps too beneficial. The latter type leaves the reader in a state where it is uncertain if the apparently good anomaly will develop into something terrifying and evil; the reader will wonder whether the story will resolve itself in one of two typical ways. Of course, as the inverted classic became in turn a well-worn formula, its value as a means to frustrate and violate expectations diminished. The SF reader simply had another pattern of expectations he could bring to the fiction.

This sort of tension seems hardly enough, then, to sustain an entire sub-group of SF. The inverted story had to work through some other aesthetic devices, had to find its artistic fulfillment through some other ploy than by merely exploiting its similarity to the standard status quo formula. And indeed it did. The main method of creating interest is through the depiction of the anomaly. Since the anomaly is positive and is something that supposedly does not presently exist in society, the story must somehow be contrived in an artful way, for useful things that can be explained in rational (rather than, say, magical) ways should already be present in society as it stands, and their absence (or nonexistence) should somehow be explained.

By undertaking this formula, the writer presents himself with a puzzle: how to convincingly depict an anomaly that is at once positive, plausible, and certain to be rejected by familiar society. Unfortunately, this is a puzzle that writers generally were unable (or unwilling) to solve. The positive anomalies their stories showed were invariably ones readers had to take on faith. The Manna, the Coultonite, the psycho-tector, and even atomic power were, quite simply, fabricated. Such stories push against the margins of the status quo formula, and suggest that the realm of SF is not always limited to showing familiar reality in an affirming light. The inverted status quo formula points to other forms—notably, subversive SF, in which the typical world of the thirties is usurped and undercut.

THE STATUS QUO FORMULA TODAY: *ALIEN*

Since the 1930s the status quo formula has been employed most frequently in television and movie SF. The variety most routinely employed has been the transplanted type. With its emphasis on exotic settings and situations, but its continual assertion of the familiar, the transplanted variety of status quo tale has proven a durable framework for movies such as *Star Wars,* and television series like "Space: 1999" and "Star Trek." These examples of the formula closely conform to the status quo pattern because the same heroes must return next week (in the case of television) or for the sequel (in the movies). The science fiction, in these examples, is only a device to make the standard popular culture fare a little different. Hence, television shows like "Battlestar Galactica" are indeed no more than "Bonanza" in space. Little attention is paid to using the SF element in any way other than as a device which provokes a conflict. This conflict resolves itself in much the same way week after week or movie after movie.

Yet there is another major reason that status quo SF has appeared in such garb and with such depressing frequency. It is still the ideal form to conflate a number of popular genres and therefore appeal to a large audience. *Alien,* a movie that appeared in the summer of 1979, was a huge box office success, grossing $4.7 million in its first week.[34] It uses a number of popular motifs—notably those from science fiction, horror, and pornographic narratives—and serves them to the audience in a relentless, fast-paced fashion. If a science fiction-like scene is not on screen, then a horror one is; and in both types of scenes, subtle sexual images prevail. Director Ridley Scott has found the ideal vehicle for bringing together three powerful sets of images.

The horror elements, for example, can be found in many movies, regardless of their setting. Director Ridley Scott remarks, "The film happens to be set in space but really it's a film about terror. It could have been an old cargo ship in the South Seas with a crew of seven that lands on an island, encounters a horror of some kind, and then can't get [it] off."[35] *Alien* concerns a crew of seven workers in space who answer a distress call on a distant planet, and then inadvertently take an alien life form aboard their spaceship. Conventional shock tactics are used; the monster is hiding in the complex webwork of machinery within the space-ship *Nostromo,* and it leaps out and devours various members of the crew. The effect is indeed frightening, as are the effects of any kind of "haunted house" movie. They depend for their impact in no way upon the spaceship setting.

One particularly successful strategy Scott uses to heighten the monster's horror is to make its shape difficult to determine. First, the audience is never given a good look at the alien; its head and jaws are flashed on the screen so quickly that they almost bypass conscious apprehension. Many horror films rely on similar strategies; the shark in *Jaws*, for example, is not shown onscreen until the second half of the movie. Scott intensifies the efficacy of such a ploy by making the monster-alien change, too. It has five distinct forms, from the small neonate monster, to the black, long-tailed hominid of the final sequence. In between these two forms, the audience has little idea of the shape or size of the monster. Combine this ignorance of the monster's form with the constant fear of an unsuspected attack, and the effect is very horrific indeed.

The way science fictional elements are handled complements the horror mode. In a transplanted status quo story, the science fiction elements work on two levels: the "transplanted" or future version of reality that is only a disguise for our reality is one level of change. The story usually displays some environmental, technological, or biological anomaly (an other-worldly setting, spaceships traveling at the speed of light, an alien among the crew like "Star Trek's" Mr. Spock). The conflict in such stories is provided by the introduction of some even more strange and unfamiliar element. In *Alien,* both of these SF aspects transport the viewer to a realm that is not only different or anomalous, but also quite terrifying. There is little illumination in this movie, but many scenes of terror.

The transplanted reality, for example, is presented to the viewer via various forms of sensory bombardment. The opening sequences use a soundtrack that almost completely obfuscates any onscreen conversation: the soundtrack employs various groans, buzzes, foghorn-like noises, and mechanical sounds that suggest a very different kind of environment, or at least total immersion in one that is strange and threatening. A computer room that the commander regularly visits is a small cubicle filled with hundreds of lights; like the character inside this room, the audience, too, feels surrounded by lights that flash on and off in no predictable or understandable way. The effect of combining these audience-overwhelming special and audio effects with a sense of routine 1979 reality merely transplanted is to remove the audience (along with the crew in the story) from the known and the familiar, thrusting them into a world of flashing lights and a cacophony of buzzing, clicking sounds that frightens through disorientation.

The tension between these two elements of the transplanted reality—the familiar and the unknown—is one that director Scott carefully contrives. There must be enough of the familiar, contemporary world so that the audience cares about what happens, and there must also be enough that is exotic so that the soon-to-be introduced SF element seems plausible. Despite the futuristic technology that the *Nostromo* represents, complete with suspended animation chamber and computer room, there are reminders of the twentieth-century world. The workers on the ship argue about overtime, for example; and when the ranking female officer (Sigourney Weaver) takes command, she is for some reason less authoritative than the male commander. Obviously, the future world is still a sexist one. Yaphet Kotto wears a headband recalling the one he wore in a very different movie, *Blue Collar*; the other maintenance worker wears a hat with a bill. In a sense, the crew of seven seems very much like a group of everyday, normal people transplanted to the belly of an immensely complex spaceship, and even on this level there are, expectedly, some tense moments merely handling the awesomeness of the technology that is common to the future world.

The anomaly encountered by this crew is basically two fold. First, they inadvertently take an alien aboard the ship. This alien is a highly adaptive life form which apparently enters one of the crewmember's bodies, gestates within him, and then erupts from his chest. In keeping with the movie's attempt to shock and dislocate the viewer, this birth is from the belly of a man, and is as unexpected as it is grisly. The monster then hides in the ship, grows, kills people, is apparently impervious to the crew's efforts to combat it, and seems indestructible. It has remarkable similarities to A. E. Van Vogt's Coeurl in "Black Destroyer" (see pp. 57-59) which, like the alien, is destroyed through expulsion, is black, is fantastically aggressive, is nearly indestructible. Unlike Coeurl, though, the alien is never given any thought processes; the situation is never told from its point of view. Telling the tale from the alien's perspective would have diminished its capacity to stir terror. The audience is not asked to sympathize with the alien nor asked to view it as only one of life's many forms competing for limited resources. It is expected merely to be scared by it.

The second half of the anomaly encountered by the crew is the discovery that one of their number, the science officer (named Ash, and played by Ian Holm) is an android or a robot so perfectly engineered that it looks and acts human. In what will doubtless become a famous SF film sequence, this android self-destructs and, while doing so, reveals the nature of its and the *Nostromo*'s mission. They have been sent by "the Company" to collect an alien life form (now loose aboard the ship) and bring it back to be used as the "ultimate aggressive weapon." The crew is expendable. Such an explanation is basically so much flummery, tacked on as an excuse for the chills and thrills of the plot. The existence of the android, however, is intriguing. That it could have lived in the midst of the crew for so long a period of time without being detected implies the existence of a supertechology on earth that apparently operates secretly, a fact that could have frightening repercussions. Unlike the technology which, in transplanted tales, is usually part of the status quo-like reality, this android suggests that the technology is getting out of control. But this idea is not stressed.

The overriding set of images that help facilitate *Alien*'s relentless level of tension is sexual. The sexual imagery of *Alien* is, like the rest of the movie, carefully contrived. The first portion of the movie shows a large number of fairly undisguised vaginal and phallic images. Plants on the planet unfold in an obscene, sexual way; the telescope on the planet is clearly phallic, as is the newborn alien, which erupts like an instant erection from actor John Hurt's torso. In a similar vein, the alien creature that had adhered to Hurt's face for a few days seems, when it falls off, to be a disembodied pudendum. Such imagery is not coincidentally sexual. The designer of the monster and the planet, H. R. Giger, "combines organic-looking shapes (bones, sinews, tubes, reptilian creatures) into a 3-D hell of writhing misery and despair," Kirk Honeycutt reports. "Echoing both Hieronymous Bosch and Salvador Dali, his works have been described as machine-age eroticism."[36]

The film abounds not only with machine age erotic imagery but with numerous surrogate sex acts as well. As it moves into the second half, the film's fairly static erotic imagery escalates into a violent surrogate sexuality, from the method by which the monster attacks (its telescoping jaws bore directly into its victims' faces) to the violent attempt by the science officer/android to force a rolled-up magazine into Sigourney Weaver's mouth. Unlike pornographic movies in which the sex act is repeated time after time in endless, exhausting permutations, *Alien* titillates and suggests throughout. The nudity and sexuality of the final scene, in which Weaver slowly disrobes, are therefore effectively climactic. Weaver, the main female sexual force, is to have the inevitable natural showdown with the aggressively male sexual force, the alien. Wearing only white underwear, she confronts the alien in its final, homonid form, its black tail threateningly phallic, its telescoping, penetrating jaws bigger than ever. Ridley Scott remarks on the absence of overt sexuality in *Alien*: "There was a scene in the script where one of the women goes up to find Tom Skerritt staring at the stars. She says 'I need relief,' and you know what she's asking for. It was a good scene, but I never shot it because it suddenly didn't have any place in the film."[37] Indeed, the less mention there is of the sex act, the more effective is the subliminal sensual bombardment and the more easily sustained the level of sexual tension.

The success of *Alien* testifies, better than anything, to the malleability of the status quo form of science fiction. Originally emerging as a spin-off from other popular genres such as the detective and the western, the status quo variety, in 1979, can find its expression through film technology. In fact, such space age technology can disguise the routineness of the story being offered, and can make a movie like *Alien,* clothed in "machine-age erotica," highly successful. The status quo form still draws upon a number of popular modes and still relies for its impact on action/adventure sequences. The basic potentialities that 30s SF writers strove for are to be found in this new, glossy update, though. The transplanted reality comes very close to being destroyed entirely; only one crew member survives to defeat the monster. Social taboos are flouted throughout, from the curiously confused sexuality of a man being invaded by an alien seed and giving birth, to suggested robot-human and alien-human sexual coupling. And the attractiveness of the evil is suggested as well; the idea of an immeasurably aggressive/sexual being that leaves behind itself a constant stream of viscous fluid represents an ultra "machismo" type of masculinity that is both horrifying and grotesquely attractive. Finally, though, the status quo structure in *Alien* serves the same basic function it served in the thirties pulps: it brings the unknown under control, and molds it into the clichés of familiar narrative sequences. Just as in the thirties fears of the "Yellow Peril," hormone experimentation, and the takeover of technology were assuaged by much of magazine SF, so in *Alien* are 70s anxieties allayed. Such issues as secret weapon development by the government and recombinant DNA research, though not directly mentioned in the film, are suggested and defused by *Alien*. They are simplified to the level of a basic haunted-house conflict, and reified in the "person" of the alien itself. "Pluck and luck" win out in the end though the victory is inevitably pyrrhic. Even the complex psychosexual issues the film touches upon are expelled at the conclusion along with the monster.

It is fortunate for science fiction that a number of other formulas evolved during the thirties, and that the genre still produces less manipulative and less simpleminded works than *Alien*. Movie and television SF seem approximately forty years behind written SF. It is to be hoped that the gap between the media closes somewhat, so that more serious science fiction can take advantage of the many excellent technical effects now available.

NOTES

1. John G. Cawelti, *Adventure, Mystery, and Romance* (Chicago: Univ. of Chicago Press, 1976), pp. 82-83.

2. Nat Schachner, "Ancestral Voices," *Astounding Stories,* Dec. 1933, p. 71. Throughout, the format for citing from the pulp magazines will be as follows: the first reference will be footnoted, though there will be a parenthetical notation of the date and magazine being referred to. The abbreviations used will be: *AS* for *Astounding Stories* of *Astounding Stories of Super Science*. From January, 1930 to March, 1933, the magazine kept the longer title. With the October, 1933 issue, the "of Super Science" portion was dropped. When Campbell took over the editorship in 1938, he renamed the magazine *Astounding Science Fiction*, starting with the March, 1938 issue. These issues will be abbreviated as *ASF*. Other pulps will be abbreviated in similar ways: *Wonder Stories* as *WS; Amazing Stories as AMZ; Amazing Quarterly* as *AMQ*.

3. Ainslee Jenkins, "In the Shadow of the Tii," *Astounding Stories,* Nov. 1933, p. 45.

4. Edmond Hamilton, "The Monsters of Mars," *Astounding Stories of Super Science,* Apr. 1931, p. 4.

5. Thornton Ayre, "Penal World," *Astounding Stories,* Oct. 1937, p. 110.

6. Paul Ernst, "The 32nd of May," *Astounding Stories,* Apr. 1935, p. 113.

7. Douglas Drew, "Nightmare Island," *Astounding Stories,* Oct. 1936, p. 122.

8. John D. Clark, "Minus Planet," *Astounding Stories,* Apr. 1937, p. 88.

9. Tom Curry, "From an Amber Block," *Astounding Stories of Super Science,* July 1930, p. 61.

10. Arthur Burks, "Manape the Mighty," *Astounding Stories of Super Science,* June 1931, p. 314.

11. Nat Schachner, "The 100th Generation," *Astounding Stories,* May 1934, p. 88.

12. Donald Day, *Index to the Science Fiction Magazines 1926-50* (Portland, Oregon: Perri Press, 1952), p. 38.

13. Spencer Lane, "Origin of Thought," *Astounding Science Fiction,* July 1938, p. 100.

14. A. E. Van Vogt, "Black Destroyer," *Astounding Science Fiction,* July 1939, p. 9.

15. Gary Gerani and Paul H. Schulman, *Fantastic Television* (New York: Harmony Books, 1977), p. 107.

16. Stanley G. Weinbaum, "Parasite Planet," *Astounding Stories,* Feb. 1935, p. 56.

17. See Appendix under Gilmore, Anthony for the dates and titles of the "Hawk Carse" stories (they are starred).

18. Clifford D. Simak, "Hellhounds of the Cosmos," *Astounding Stories of Super Science*, June 1932, uses this format.

19. C. L. Moore, "Shambleau," in *The Best of C. L. Moore,* ed. Lester del Rey (New York: Ballantine, 1975), pp. 2-3.

20. Owen Wister, *The Virginian* (1902; rpt. New York: Pocket, 1974), p. 3.

21. See pp. 11-20 of Michael Resnick, *Official Guide to the Fantastics* (Florence, Ala.: House of Collectibles, 1976). The hero plus were basically a mid-to-late thirties phenomenon. Some dates of the hero pulps: *The Avenger*—1939-42; *Doc Savage*—1933-49; *G-8 And His Battle Aces*—1933-44; *Ki-Gor*—1939-54; *Operator #5*—1934-39; *The Shadow*—1931-49; *The Spider*—1933-43.

22. Some examples are Anthony Gilmore's "Hawk Carse" stories; Sewall Peaslee Wright's "Commander John Hanson" stories; Kent Casey's "Dr. Von Theil" stories; C. L. Moore's "Northwest Smith" and "Jirel of Joiry" stories; S. P. Meek's "Dr. Bird" stories. Most of these series were not, surprisingly, limited to one magazine each. See Day for complete lists of each series.

23. Leslie Johnson and Eric Frank Russell, "Seeker of To-Morrow," *Astounding Stories,* July 1937, p. 140.

24. Raymond Z. Gallun, "Hotel Cosmos," *Astounding Science Fiction,* July 1938, p. 142.

25. Cawelti, pp. 80-98.

26. Donald Wandrei, "Murray's Light," *Astounding Stories,* June 1935, p. 34.

27. Stanton A. Coblentz, "Manna from Mars," *Astounding Stories,* Mar. 1934, p. 46.

28. Nat Schachner, "The Ultimate Metal," *Astounding Stories,* Feb. 1935, p. 95.

29. John Jessel (pseud.), "The Adaptive Ultimate," *Astounding Stories,* Nov. 1935, p. 114.

30. A. T. Locke, "The Machine That Knew Too Much," *Astounding Stories,* Dec. 1933, p. 38.

31. Stanton A. Coblentz, "The Truth About the Psycho-Tector," *Astounding Stories,* Oct. 1934, p. 87.

32. Charles Willard Diffin, "The Power and the Glory," *Astounding Stories of Super Science,* July 1930, p. 106.

33. Don A. Stuart (pseud.), "Elimination," *Astounding Stories,* May 1936, p. 46.

34. Kirk Honeycutt, "Director of 'Alien' Launches Cold Terror Into Outer Space," *Minneapolis Star,* 25 June 1979, p. 1C.

35. Honeycutt, p. 4C.

36. Honeycutt, p. 4C. For more examples of Giger's erotic imagery, see H. R. Giger, "H. R. Giger's Alien Encounters," *Penthouse,* April 1980, pp. 142-53.

37. Honeycutt, p. 1C.

3.
Subversive Science Fiction

INTRODUCTION

Science fiction split radically from other popular forms as the thirties progressed. By the late thirties, the status quo formula was less common in the pages of *Astounding,* while the other science fiction magazines continued to embrace that simplistic formula. One major dimension of the evolution of science fiction was the emergence of what I call the "subversive" formula. This variety opens with a brief picture of familiar social reality or of a reality slightly transplanted out of the ordinary. Sometimes this picture will be only implied, so that the story opens with what must have been, to most readers, the focal point of their interest: the conflict between familiar reality and some anomaly inserted into it. Throughout the story, action focuses on the battle between the anomalous and the familiar, much as it does in the status quo form. But in the subversive formula the anomaly is absorbed or incorporated into familiar reality. The pattern of action can be diagrammed thus:

Reality ⟶ Anomaly ⟶ A vs. R ⟶ A New Version
(often implied)   (A)   of Reality

The anomaly may be regarded as a threat or boon. It may subvert a portion of society. It may destroy society. It may improve a segment of society or, in the utopian version, lead to a revolutionary improvement in the whole of society. Unlike almost all other popular genres, this type of SF does not leave the status quo intact, but usurps it, alters it, effects in it a mutation that could never be accommodated by the conventional-value-affirming, conservative slant the public had come to recognize in other popular fiction.

This variety of a popular genre did not, of course, emerge instantaneously from the mass of more routine fiction, nor did it immediately appear in its purest form. Frequently, for example, a subversive tale will closely resemble a status quo formula story in that, throughout, some agent or character will be striving to oust the anomaly or restore the world to its more familiar form. The ending will often demonstrate such resistant actions to be against the grain of the depicted popular opinion: most of society embraces the change. Only the ending in this type of story surprises the reader—the entire early portion of the tale reads very much like those status quo tales which had become so familiar to most people.[1]

Radical departures from usual pulp patterns were strongly discouraged by the publishing industry. Publishers and editors felt that, to hold their segment of the pulp-reading population, they had to publish fiction similar to that which had sold in the past. Therefore, SF writers developed a set of conventions that disguised the fact that they were doing something very different from the norm. One such tactic was framing the subversive story, making it a tale within a tale, so that its structure closely resembled that of status quo SF. By using this ploy, a story could have a central tale that depicted an entirely subverted or destroyed reality, without in fact offering a substantial threat to the contemporary status quo of the frame. L. Sprague deCamp's "The Blue Giraffe" (*ASF,* August 1939), for example, opens with Athelstan Cuff assuaging his foster son's insecurities. The boy had been crying, he tells Cuff, because "some of the guys say you aren't really my father."[2] Cuff then tells a long, elaborate tale about biological mutations, a race of human-like baboons, and blue giraffes. He claims he could not father any children because he, too, was subject to some ray that caused biological mutation: the boy's initial discomfort about being adopted is thereby defused. H. G. Wells's *The Time Machine* takes such a form as well: the comfortable Victorian drawing room it opens on appears to be the same at the end. The Time Traveller himself disappears down the corridors of the future. The distorted Englands he confronts clearly subvert conventional notions about social organization, but such future visions can be set aside as ones that pose no immediate threat. His tale can be written off as a form of madness that has no basis in fact, no witness to swear to it, no incontrovertible proofs of its veracity. Such a framing structure allowed writers to be as pessimistic as they wanted; they could subvert or denigrate reality in any number of ways so long as the stories ended in the same reassuring way in which they began.

Like the formulas discussed throughout this book, this story-formula is somewhat fluid, less fixed and quantified than the equation of it suggests. It can, however, be most readily identified in a story by the picture of a society very much like our own being subtly, partially, or entirely undermined, and changing in ways so that there is no turning back. Conventional reality is shown adapting or surrendering to the anomaly. This society-altering interaction is what distinguishes the subversive form from other forms. The transplanted status quo, by contrast, while resembling the subversive tale, stresses not so much our society (or a version of it) actively accommodating an anomaly, but the elimination of any threat to that transplanted status quo. In the other world formula an entirely anomalous world is posited and any interaction between it and an agent of the contemporary or familiar world must be implied. The subversive form is unique among popular fiction because its end product is the result of society's blending with something previously alien to it.

Often, in this version, the status quo is virtually destroyed. Holocaust tales were fairly common in the thirties, depicting massive destruction and usually a rebuilding of the decimated society. Usually the blame for the destruction is placed on one weak element of existent social reality—for instance, poor defense, or failure to heed scientists' warnings. Seldom do stories of this variety demonstrate multiple weaknesses in society; the full-fledged oppressive world like that found in *1984* or *Brave New World* does not often appear in the thirties pulps. There is little doubt, however, in stories of this kind, that the destroyed society brought about its own destruction.

Many stories of the subversive variety show not the destruction of a familiar reality but the incorporation of something anomalous into it. Such stories have a paradoxical focus. By depicting a change or anomaly absorbed in a beneficial way, the status quo is allowed to maintain its integrity. The accommodation is so convincing and complete that in some cases this formula could be said to resemble the standard status quo formula. A group of scientists, for example, could be shown trying to control a robot suddenly possessed of the power of independent thought. In a status quo treatment such a robot would be deprogrammed or destroyed (as in Eando Binder's "Orestes Revolts," *ASF*, October 1938), while in a subversive tale this robot might be shown being brought under control only temporarily. Society might need such awesome robots who have the power of independent thought—to explore other worlds, for example.[3] Such a necessity tells much about society, and not all of what it does say is reassuring, no matter how marvelous the invention or familiar the setting. The equilibrium that has been reached in this type of story is a new one, and implies not only a sense of instability, but a feeling that the old equilibrium was somehow lacking. SF writers of the thirties (and many since) exploit this tension between the incorporated subversive element and the overall loss of previous lifestyle, knowledge, or social pattern that such a subversion inevitably brings.

Oftentimes elements of a utopia intrude into such stories in the form of a small group of people, for example, who share remarkable powers or values, or in the form of specific inventions. Yet the utopic potential of this formula is seldom stressed in any concerted way. It is difficult to postulate a full-fledged utopia when the premise is that a comfortably familiar reality is being juxtaposed with a new version of itself. Though the new version may have improvements, it is also—because of its strangeness— almost always threatening.

In the subversive formula, society itself becomes a character. This "large view" contrasts with that of the status quo formula, in which the reader's attention is basically focused on the fate of individuals, through whom society's fate can be inferred. "Easy-Goin'" Dave Ledrack restores order in "Hotel Cosmos," and all is well in that world. The status of any final order in subverted tales, on the other hand, is problematic, and must be inferred from the story's events and resolution rather than from a single character's situation. This final order reflects back on society's capacity to evolve, or undergo change.

As might be expected, subversive tales often had left-wing political undertones. Many of the active thirties SF fans were very politically oriented; in fact, they divided up basically into two groups: the Michelists (or Communists) and a more conservative faction, the International Scientific Association, led by Will Sykora.[4] A large number of subversive stories show the incorporation of communal societies or the embracing of alien life forms. Many fans disliked this emphasis, and saw SF only as a means of stirring up interest in science. The important thing to note, however, is not so much the petty fan wars and factionalism, but the kind of SF that emerged from them and continues to flourish today.

SUBVERSIVE SCIENCE FICTION— DESTRUCTIVE VARIETY

Perhaps the simplest and most straightforward way in which 1930s SF writers depicted their reality "subverted" was by showing it destroyed. An early version of the currently popular "disaster thriller," destructive/subversive SF deals in a whole range of social disasters—from earth-devastating holocausts to the creation of insidious monsters. The new version of society this variety offers is invariably a bleak, pessimistic one. The fact that the tale itself can be told suggests the existence of survivors or a fictive frame of some sort: a modest hope. But such tales are essentially cautionary. They warn the public, point up some highly dangerous feature in society, and extrapolate from it to show possible destructive outcomes. In the process there are occasions for lots of action: massive battles, poignant love-scenes, murderous gangs, mutilations, pestilence, depravity—in short, all the trappings of the war story. Indeed, it is the final war, the true "war to end all wars," that SF writers working in this mode depict.

A slightly less insistent incarnation of this formula shows social reality not destroyed utterly, but vastly altered for the worse. Society is undermined to such an extent that it seems to resemble no known reality; and in this variety, society's guise indicates a decadence or dissolution. Throughout, there is some agent of a known reality, or some recent memory of conventional reality, or, perhaps, some juxtaposed version of it, that always serves as an implied contrast to this new, "decadent" offshoot. This juxtaposition highlights the poignancy of the change, stresses the sense of loss. In Stanton A. Coblentz's "Triple-Geared" (*AS*, April 1935), for example, the narrator is a man who has returned to New York City after ten years' absence. He discovers that the entire populace is addicted to "Speedo," a drug that increases metabolism three-fold. He meets another person not taking the drug (a poet, significantly), and together they confront the weird anomaly-stricken world. Throughout, their opinion forms the basis for judging this new world. There is often, in this variety, a suggestion that the dissolution need not necessarily take place: in "Triple-Geared," people can simply desist from taking Speedo. In other stories, the anomaly is only one of many possible futures or, perhaps, a metaphoric version of how contemporary reality itself operates. Such a suggestion naturally softens the impact of the story, and makes it more closely resemble the status quo tale.

The destructive/subversive form focuses not so much on the plausibility of the change it projects—invasion from space, assumption of some humanity-sapping technology, emergence of weird, destructive biologies—as on the reaction of the social system to such changes. It shows society under enormous stress, and the evil forced to the surface by this stress. The change or anomaly itself acts as a device to uncover weaknesses in the status quo. This weakness will sometimes be society's susceptibility to certain kinds of apparently attractive technologies (like Speedo). More often, in this variety, the weakness shown will be a result of the world being under especial duress, the usual popular literature violence and action, cast in "scientific" or futuristic terms and carrying a sense of unprecedented, huge-scale, awful destruction. "Rebirth," by Thomas Calvert McClary (*AS*, February-March 1934), starts with thirties reality: "The city hit its normal workday stride. A few people fired, fewer hired."[5] Into this world, an outside agent intrudes: "The death of memory and habit." The entire two-part story shows how mankind is basically greedy, unpleasant, warlike, lustful. The plausibility of the anomaly is never at issue; what causes the conflict and excitement are man's presumed weaknesses.

The reason such a form logically emerges in the SF pulps is that destruction/dissolution/holocaust are usually threatened though never fully enacted in the early status quo variety of SF. Subversive/destructive SF arose to keep alive the threat that status quo forms offered. If every thirties SF story showing a potentially destructive anomaly ended with that destructive force being expelled, the genre would certainly have stagnated. The destructive/subversive form, by keeping alive the potency of the "evil anomaly," lent a depth and complexity to the straight status quo story. With the regular appearance in the SF pulps of these two complementary varieties of stories, readers could better appreciate the tension that introduction of a threatening anomaly could provide.

Though the same themes appear in status quo and subversive/destructive varieties of SF, the differing endings suggest very different emphases. The status quo form, for example, could have as much artistic merit as the subversive/destructive form. Sir Arthur Conan Doyle's "The Poison Belt" (1913) and Eando Binder's "Life Disinherited" (*AS*, March 1937) employ the same theme—earth is beset with a poison gas that destroys life—but in the former the status quo is restored, while in the latter three people are all that remain of civilization. Conan Doyle's story, which was not reprinted in the pulps (probably because it was always available in hard cover), shows a group, having provided themselves with oxygen, surviving the poison gas, and exploring the decimated world after the gas has dissipated. But the effects of this gas are only temporary, and the world reawakens the next day, having no recollection of any loss. Such a story calls into question the utility of scientific prediction and suggests a benign pattern beneath the obvious physical landscape. "What will not be forgotten," an article in the *Times* proclaims at the end of the story, "and what will and should continue to obsess our imaginations, is this revelation of the possibilities of the universe, this destruction of our ignorant self-complacency, and this demonstration of how narrow is the path of our material existence and what abysses may lie upon either side of it."[6] Binder's story, on the other hand, also shows scientists trying to warn the populace, but the warning goes unheeded, and the human race essentially passes away. The suggestion it makes seems less sophisticated than that of the earlier story: People should listen to those who know; if they fail to, they will die.

One major difference between the two stories—and between the status quo and subversive varieties of SF—is that Conan Doyle's discredits the anomaly. Like a dream, the anomaly is something soon forgotten and, finally, difficult to authenticate. The later story, however simpleminded its point, nonetheless ends by questioning the validity of a social order wherein scientists, for example, have no voice. In addition, closing as it does—showing the characters eating a meal of canned food—it takes seriously the subversive ability of certain eventualities: if the status quo story resembles a dream, the subversive tale resembles a nightmare.

The major difference between the status quo and subversive forms, the conclusion, can take four basic forms. A framing device (similar to the one in "The Blue Giraffe") can bring the reader both into and out of a destructive subversive tale. An enclave ending is fairly common in this form—humanity survives in a very confined area and consists of a small number of doomed individuals (as in "Life Disinherited"). The "decadent society" ending, such as that in "Triple-Geared," also appears regularly: the status quo reality has been undermined to such an extent that the society left at the end is only a flawed caricature of what it once was. A final variety is the sinister "monster is on the loose" type, as found in Donald Wandrei's "A Scientist Divides" (*AS*, September 1934). The scientist of this tale creates a serum that, "Blob"-like, absorbs living tissue and then divides. The serum takes over its inventor, escapes, and terrorizes the countryside. "There is nothing more to add," the narrator remarks near the end of the story, "there is nothing that I or anyone can do, now. . . ."[7] Often these endings will be combined in various ways. The story within the frame could, for example, show humanity surviving through only a few members, or could show some awful evil loose in the world.

Many other combinations are, of course, possible; many were tried. Though the aesthetic potentialities of the subversive tale are similar to those of the status quo variety, its final success or failure depends on the ending, or the final subverted vision. How convincing is the new, transmuted status quo? How convincing is the transition from the entirely familiar world into the strange or anomalous? The weaknesses causing society's subversion must be both convincing and appropriate enough so that the social process displayed will seem not only to move easily into its subverted state but also to contain within it the mechanisms of its own dissolution. Society should seem to bring the downfall upon itself. In the following section, I will examine "Twilight," a science fiction story in this mode that is successful in both its elaboration of the completely subverted state and in the connection it makes to the status quo from which that state emerged.

"TWILIGHT"

John W. Campbell, the man who took over the editorship of *Astounding Stories* in late 1937 and brought it into the early 70s, was a well-respected SF author in his own right during the thirties. Though his early stories ["The Mightiest Machine" (*AS*, December 1934); "The Black Star Passes" (*AMQ*, Fall 1930); "The Last Evolution" (*AMZ*, August 1932)] were popular with fans, his mid-to-late thirties tales, written under the pseudonym Don A. Stuart, are probably his most accomplished. Alva Rogers marks 1934 as an important year in SF largely because, in November, *Astounding* printed "Twilight" under the Stuart byline. The year 1934 "introduced Don A. Stuart with the classic 'Twilight,' an event of far-reaching significance for, as Campbell said in the introduction of his first Don A. Stuart collection: 'It led to the development of the Don A. Stuart stories, and thus to the modern *Astounding*.'"[8] "Twilight" was nothing less than the successful emergence of a new kind of SF: the destructive subversive variety. Here was a story that was compelling and entertaining, but was markedly different from almost all the SF that had preceded it.

The major focus of "Twilight" is earth of the year A.D. 7 million. The globe is devoid of all but human life, and humans are entirely dependent on machines. Such a vision alone was not new to 30s readers. The future supercivilization appeared in some tales by Arthur J. Burks (*Earth the Marauder, AS,* July-September 1930) and Ray Cummings (*The Exile of Time, AS,* April-July 1931), and in many others. What was new in "Twilight," however, was the relentless subversion of highly positive, exciting visions by negative, destructive ones. In previous stories about future machine-dominated societies, the values presented were straightforward: certain social arrangements were debilitating for humanity; others were good. Usually this clear-cut value judgment allowed for a clean break with the imagined world in the form of a return to the conventional, familiar status quo. The imagined world was either "too good for" humanity as we know it, or it was something any sane person would want nothing to do with. In either event, it could be readily abandoned—after a thoroughgoing exploration—by the author and characters. "Twilight" uses an ambiguous and highly convincing mix of the attractive and the destructive to make its future vision seem somehow inevitable—no dream world to blithely tour and forget, but a version of social reality that had a completeness and depth to it that could not be denied.

The theme of the evil beneath the good, or the familiar and hopeful tainted with the alien and the inhuman, is a common one in Campbell's work. His famous story, "Who Goes There?" (*ASF*, August 1938), which was made into the movie *The Thing* (1951), depicts a monster from another world taking over the bodies of men on an antarctic expedition. The action involves differentiating the human members of the expedition from those who have been taken over. Sam Moskowitz has an interesting, inventive psychobiographical explanation of Campbell's use of the "evil beneath the apparently good" theme. John W. Campbell had been raised by a mother who was indistinguishable from her identical twin sister, the author's aunt. Frequently, young John would come home to confront a woman he thought was his loving, affectionate mother, only to discover—sooner or later—that she was his bitter, unkind aunt. This oft-repeated experience translated itself, Moskowitz suggests, into Campbell's fiction, in which the apparently good or positive is actually menacing and alien at the core.[9]

No matter how convincing such an explanation is, however, it seems ultimately somewhat reductive. "Twilight" is more than a recasting or reification of its author's childhood anxieties and traumas: the dream world of the future insidiously subverted by nightmare was obviously as compelling to Depression-era readers as it is to readers today. It is more useful to perceive "Twilight" (and Campbell's other works) as a vision of thirties and post-thirties society. The widespread appeal of Campbell's stories and of the brand of SF he fostered and printed in *Astounding* from 1937 to 1971 suggest that story patterns like the one used in "Twilight" had significance beyond the merely psychobiographical.

Campbell's stories and editing brought to the fore the kind of SF that this one story represents, depicting the world and its status quo being subverted as a result of their flaws.

There are three levels to "Twilight"; it is a story within a story within a story. The narrator—who is never named—tells a story which his friend Jim Bendell, a real estate salesman, has related to him. Bendell had picked up a hitchhiker, Ares Sen Kenlin, a scientist from A.D. 3059. The latter had been traveling in time. Kenlin's tale of his visit to the year 7 million forms the bulk of the text. Though this structure effectively separates the vision of A.D. 7 million from the status quo reality of real estate men and hitchhikers—buffering the 1930s reader through the use of intervening fictions—it also serves to make the connection between three distinct levels of civilization (1932, 3059, and 7 million), each displacing the earlier level. It is a structure which promises a great deal—at least fictive voyages to two future time periods. But finally, it suggests that the operating principles in these time zones are the same: possibility, hope, and enlightenment are subverted in all three.

The story Ares Sen Kenlin tells of the year 7 million is necessarily distorted. He is from A.D. 3059 and is less awed by supertechnology than the man of 1932. But he is awed by much of the world he sees in the far future, a world of infinite sources of power and food, of interplanetary travel, of an artificial "soft, silvery light, slightly rose," but most of all of "wondrous perfect machines."[10] "When earth is cold, and the Sun has died out, those machines will go on. When earth begins to crack and break, those perfect, ceaseless machines will try to repair her" (p. 48). Kenlin rides a marvelous airship that can perceive obstacles he cannot, that travels with unbelievable speed but has neutralized acceleration so that a trip from Boston to Washington takes three minutes. In short, it is a technological wonderland of the sort familiar to science fiction readers. What is unusual, however, is the race of people living within it: "For the one thing that had made man great had left him. As I looked into their faces and eyes on landing I knew it. . . . They were not curious! Man had lost the instinct of curiosity!" (p. 55). There is not a race of beings to succeed men; they have killed off everything save the plants, "and man was too far along to bring intelligence and mobility from the plants.

Perhaps he could have in his prime" (p. 55). It is a world of miracles that Kenlin describes, but it is deflated by the sacrifices man has had to make to get so far: such a world, Campbell suggests, saps man of his humanity, and separates him from any experience but a mechanical, synthetic one. The implication is that by solving the world's technical problems, humankind has lost all occasion for creative thought.

The world of 3059, Kenlin's own world, though bright and glossy on the outside, is somehow flawed. Its discovery of time travel and genetic engineering foreshadow the world of 7 million, in which there is too much technology. Kenlin is himself described in Apollo-like terms: "His features were delicate, but tremendously impressive; his eyes were gray, like etched iron, and bigger than mine—a lot. . . . His arms were long and muscled smoothly as an Indian's. . . . But he was magnificent. Most wonderful man I ever saw" (p. 46). He is, however, a prototype of the men who have made the machine world: "My father was a scientist," he explains, "in human genetics. I myself am an experiment. He proved his point, and all the world followed suit. I was the first of a new race" (p. 46). He can do amazing things, intellectually and physically, but these powers are undercut by the end product of such a "new" race: futilely laboring machines. Kenlin is indeed a supreme example of man's evolution, but his genetically engineered creation foreshadows the entire loss of a natural, human reality, a loss that the world of A.D. 7 million represents.

The depicted reality of December 9, 1932—the date Bendell picks up Kenlin on the side of the road—is also one in which flaws hide just beneath the surface. Bendell begins relating his story with a laugh "that wasn't a real laugh" but gets immediately sidetracked into talking about hitchhikers. "Most of them tell you how they lost their good jobs and tried to find work out here in the wide spaces of the West. They don't seem to realize how many people we have out here. They think all this great beautiful country is uninhabited" (p. 45). In this society even the best opportunities are arid, and people's dreams are spoiled, or their first impressions misapprehensions. The narrator even recalls when "Bendell thought the rattlesnake was a stick of wood and wanted to put it on the fire" (p. 45). The world of 1932, too, prefigures the future worlds of "Twilight."

In fact, these future worlds refer directly back to 1932, and are versions of it. For the future in which genetic engineering is possible, when the brilliant, handsome, muscular individual is the norm, and the future in which man has no worries about energy, food, or the like, are dreams that would likely be as compelling to a 1930s audience as they are to one from the early 1980s. What Campbell suggests in "Twilight" is that such dreams are unproductive ones, ill thought out, and inappropriate to mankind's best interests. And in a sense the world of 1932 may have seemed like "Twilight" to the people who lived at that time: enormous technological advancements since 1900 had created—as they had for the beings of the story's A.D. 7 million—unemployment and despair.

"Twilight" makes a comment on science fiction of the time as well; it demonstrates that the developments and advances SF stories show should not be easily accepted by readers. Campbell wrote an editorial in June, 1938, remarking that mankind advances slowly so that advancements do not seem so striking when they do occur, and much of his fiction examines the implied world surrounding such advancements.[11] Will Sykora, the fan who in 1939 declared, "Let us hope that what we read in SF may one day become reality," was in a sense pre-Campbellian, and had failed to see that human enterprise works in interrelated systems, and that technological advances could threaten humanity. Campbell—with "Twilight" and stories like it—demonstrated the possibility of such subversion, and helped bring science fiction out of the realm of speculation, wishful thinking, and self-affirmation, and into a commentary on the function and process of society.

SUBVERSIVE SCIENCE FICTION: INCORPORATIVE VARIETY

One of the most important varieties of science fiction to emerge from the thirties pulp magazines was the "incorporative" variety of the subversive formula. Like the destructive variety, this type also dramatizes the subversion of a status quo. But in the incorporative variety, this subversion is not evil and does not undermine society. Rather, society is shown incorporating some anomaly in a way that benefits it. There is, of course, a variety of subversion taking place as well; at the story's end a new state (not the status quo) is implied. In short, incorporative SF is a kind of literature that shows society adapting to and embracing change in positive, affirmative ways.

"Mind Over Matter" (*AS*, January 1935), for example, a story by Raymond Z. Gallun, follows the incorporative pattern very closely. A test pilot for a rocket plane company, Lloyd Jorgenson, has a personal problem: his girlfriend will not marry him unless he resigns. Yet he is a wonderfully skilled pilot, and Dr. Pierre Toussaint, an admirer, urges him not to resign. The worst seems to happen, though, as Jorgenson is mangled in a crash. Toussaint provides him with a robot body, a fact that is not revealed to the pilot until he has almost entirely recovered from the injuries sustained in the accident. Jorgenson is enraged and upset when he discovers his newly acquired steel person—it is a totally unprecedented medical procedure—but Toussaint administers him some chemical, and the pilot is less depressed. The doctor explains that he and Jorgenson will be able to find a human body for him eventually, and that they will be able to travel the solar system together. This story shows the young, athletic, courageous hero—a stereotype of thirties popular literature—destroyed. Yet his reincarnation in a massive and ugly metal body is shown in a positive, affirming way. The artificial body is, "for all one may know," the doctor remarks, "almost immortal, since it is not dependent upon a weak human body for its sustenance."[12] No metal monster, this, but an improvement upon the old flesh. Perhaps it is a useful corporeality for a rocket plane test pilot.

Society's gain is that it does not permanently lose a gifted test pilot—either to conventional domesticity or as a result of a disastrous crash. Yet there is a moral ambiguity at the end of "Mind Over Matter"—another distinguishing feature of the incorporative subversive tale. The reader is left wondering about the status of the Jorgenson-Toussaint relationship. Clearly it is less satisfactory than the one between Jorgenson and his former girlfriend. Jorgenson in effect gives up a normal sex life for a bizarre continuation of his career.

Not a great deal of this kind of SF appeared in the thirties. It was a trifle too "different" to immediately proliferate. Though it was at first only an offshoot of another type, its importance extends beyond the thirties; such SF is highly popular (and abundant) today. Some of the better 30s SF writers—L. Sprague deCamp, Lester del Rey, Jack Williamson, Raymond Z. Gallun—were attracted to the incorporative variety. It offered not just a chance to be different, to vary the usual formulas, but a chance to further escape the confines of the conventions of traditional popular literature which all the previously described types of SF relied upon. The status quo varieties, for example, share the socially affirmative, even conservative stance taken by most popular literature; destructive-subversive SF tends to focus on the kind of violence and action to be found in war, sea, air, adventure, and detective stories. It is no wonder that not a great deal of incorporative-subversive SF appeared in the pulp-magazine dominated thirties. Holocaust, evil aliens, wild robots, scientific villains, insane inventions, plagues, intergalactic wars, monsters, and the like could not really form the focus of an incorporative-subversive tale. With such thematic limitations, it is actually surprising that such a form surfaced at all.

The urgings that sparked writers of such unusual SF tales were, surprisingly, more literary than monetary, despite the fact that pulp fiction usually emerged through writers seeking to find an easy route to riches. As SF magazines multiplied and flourished in the late 30s, *Astounding* had come to distinguish itself from the others by virtue of the literary quality of its stories. Some were stylistically sophisticated (those of John W. Campbell, C. L. Moore, and Nat Schachner, for example) and some—many of the incorporative variety—shared with serious literature a moral ambiguity. There is no clear-cut division of good and evil in the incorporative tale: society as it stands in the status quo state is not the ideal one (as it seems to be in much popular literature) and the anomaly that is incorporated into it does not represent unmitigated evil or complete goodness. The depiction of the status quo is essentially more representational or "mimetic" than in usual pulp SF. The anomaly incorporated into this picture of reality is affirmative and also capable of altering the world. As such, it serves to high-light society's tolerance for change.

The kind of mainstream or literary work most clearly evoked by this form is the utopia. Incorporative SF approaches utopia in some instances—when the incorporated element is pervasive enough to affect the entire social structure. Almost always, though, only one fairly localized anomalous element is shown to be incorporated. Jorgenson's robot body in "Mind Over Matter" is merely a prototype; the story does not imply that all people in dangerous occupations (or who have been seriously injured) will have themselves fitted with more mechanical bodies.

In the destructive-subversive form, the entire world is often destroyed except for a small enclave of men and women; it is they who must carry on the business of living amid particulate radiation or a charred or frozen landscape. The implication is, however, that the only future awaiting them is an unpleasant death. The incorporative variety mimics the destructive-subversive variety more than the utopia because usually only a small group will successfully incorporate the anomalous element. Though this group will undoubtedly stand for the larger mass of humanity, it is, just the same, only a small-scale utopia, and often there are elements built into the story to suggest that such a state will not permeate the greater portion of society—at least not right away.

In Jack Williamson's story, "Born of the Sun" (*AS,* March 1934), the earth is shown to be only a huge egg that cracks open to destroy all human lives, except for those of the heroes, Foster Ross, his uncle, and June Trevor. They all escape on a rocket named the *Planet.* Foster's dying uncle declares a final faith: "Men will be parasites no longer, to be crushed like vermin by any chance tremor of the beast that bears them. In the *Planet* men are free, on their own. . . .' He seemed to like that phrase, for he whispered it again: 'On their own.'"[13] Though the story resembles the destructive variety in that the earth is destroyed, it also suggests that the earth was a flawed, limiting habitat. It is better for people that it was destroyed. Before the earth-egg split, fanatic religious groups had formed, and scientific endeavors had been sabotaged by them. Throughout, the impression is that the *Planet* is leaving a world on which man never belonged, and on which he could therefore never have thrived. The new race that June and Foster will start will be a better, stronger, more independent one. The "planet" they live on—the rocket, *Planet*—is entirely of their creation, and will not split open and cast them off. This story no doubt fulfilled the Depression-era fantasy of leaving the flawed and unpleasant world behind, and starting anew. The utopia, though, is far off.

This variety of SF commonly depicts a microcosmic universe which resembles the physically limited landscape in much mainstream fiction. The incorporative variety does not usually move in such cataclysmic modes as the status quo or the destructive formulas. Our world is not destroyed in this incorporative variety, as a rule. It is difficult, to be sure, to convincingly portray widespread change of any kind without making such change seem destructive of a status quo—and since the incorporative variety has a positive emphasis, writers have to keep the change they envision very localized. It is easier to do this than to project a viable and widely accepted huge-scale change from the status quo to another state of existence. A small-scale setting is necessary so that the incorporation of the anomaly seems plausible. Hence, the incorporated positive changes used in SF stories fall into basically three areas in the thirties pulps: stories that show a small group of people having found a utopic existence through an escape from conventional reality; stories that focus on solving a specific problem—often a psychological or personal one—through extraordinary, anomalous means; and finally, a type which has a slightly wider scope, but which is undercut by its less serious tone, that which humorously or satirically depicts a "positive" change.

The type of incorporative SF which shows a small group of individuals working toward a type of utopia is well exemplified by "The Upper Level Road" (*AS*, August 1935), written by F. Orlin Tremaine under the pseudonym Warner Van Lorne. In this story, a student tells his history professor, Gamaliel Eberhardt, "I saw that there is no reason for men to starve, or to lack work, or to worry about being unemployed, or even to work!"[14] The professor, whose name recalls Warren Gamaliel Harding's (and whose fairly conservative stance might also suggest something of Harding's "normalcy"), is brought to a strange, other-dimensional village. He must travel an "upper-level road" to get there. The existence of this village leads him to suspect that there are multiple levels throughout the world and, hence, that there might be enormous riches, free land, abundant natural resources, gainful employment for the masses. The professor remarks, too: "I see vast possibilities. . . . We can undertake even to force peace on the world when the time comes" (p. 47). But it is also revealed that one cannot cross into an "upper level" while thinking worldly thoughts. The thoughts have to be random or dream-like. The suggestion is that taking one's mind off this world's problems, or thinking in nonrational modes, will yield new insights, new ways of coping with the world. And the assumption of this new mode of perception apparently reforms people—no longer does the town drunkard lead the wastrel's life; no longer is Professor Eberhardt pompous and pedantic. By incorporating a mode of thinking that transcends usual patterns, unproductive people and, it is assumed, an unproductive world, can be made productive.

This version of the incorporative story is unconvincing. The utopic enclave is never full elaborated and, as it stands, consists of only twelve adults, all of whom have access to the usual (lower level) world. That in this situation they can be organized into a useful, unified social group is not surprising. To further undercut the effectuality of this story as a tract proposing social change, the precise nature of the change the characters carry out—this vast, positive, world change they have planned—is entirely hidden from the reader, and remains something we have to hesitantly infer. The dramatic focus of the story is on the discovery of this level, and the initial accompanying excitement. Though the status quo is tentatively and partially disrupted, there is a call for widespread subversion, but little dramatization of it: the professor's remarks, such as "the world is on the verge of a disastrous war" (p. 49), suggest the urgency of change, but not the *modus operandi*.

More convincing are the incorporative stories which depict some anomalous or bizarre science fictional solution being brought to bear on a personal or psychological problem. The restricted impact of the incorporated anomaly helps to make it believable, and the actual solution itself can be as idiosyncratic as the author likes. It is, after all, only a one-time occurrence. "Vibratory," a story also written under the Warner Van Lorne byline, but attributed by Moskowitz to Nelson Tremaine[15] (*ASF*, March 1938), concerns a loneliness he feels in this one. Such a story suggests that certain proceeds to immerse himself in his work, the creation of a vibration machine. When the machine is made, a creature somehow emerges from it. Ernst finds this creature is kind and sympathetic, and returns with it to its own world, thus escaping the isolation and loneliness he feels in this one. Such a story suggests that certain problems cannot be solved using this world's resources: there is no earthly way, perhaps, to compensate for the loss of a spouse. No regular or routine communication is established between the vibration creature's world and this one; a passageway has simply opened up under an anomalous set of circumstances.

Often stories in this mode concern body transplants (as in "Mind Over Matter"), heart transplants (as in "Cardiaca Vera" by Arch Carr for March, 1938, *ASF* or "The Emperor's Heart" by Henry J. Kostkos for the June, 1934, *AS*), and the like, responses to emergency situations that exceed the boundaries of the status quo reality's ability to handle them. Usually the anomaly incorporated in this kind of tale is a metaphoric version of some tension or anxiety, a character's fears or weakness hypostasized into an anomalous situation. In "Helen O'Loy" (*ASF*, December 1938), Lester del Rey's story of a man-made woman with whom the two main male characters fall in love, the implication is that women, as they exist, are not good enough for these men. Females are too guarrelsome and frivolous. The twin women the men have been seeing are disposed of by the second page: "I suppose, if we hadn't quarreled with them, we'd have married the twins in time. But Dave wanted to look over the latest Venus rocket attempt when his twin wanted to see a display stereo starring Larry Ainslee, and they were both stubborn. From then on, we forgot the girls and spent our evenings at home."[16] The final upshot is that one of the men, Dave, marries the robot they have created—Helen O'Loy—while the other, Phil, pines for this robot-woman all his life. A sentimental story, "Helen O'Loy" nonetheless demonstrates the failings of two men to abide by the social norms, and their desire to escape them. The story is not quite so male-centered, however, to suggest that all of society take such an option.

In "The Shadow Out of Time," (*AS*, June 1936), H. P. Lovecraft uses the individual experience of one man, Peaslee, as a gateway to a new view of history. This character, a university professor, has a gap in his memory: he cannot recall what he did during the five-year period of 1908-13. He only remembers reading and writing about occult lore and ancient, odd myths. He has dreams about alien races who can time travel, switch their minds with those of other entities and record the history of other races. The story seems, at this point, to be a psychological study, the history of one academician's problems. Yet, after publishing a paper on these dreams, Peaslee is contacted by an Australian who has found rocks and hieroglyphs telling a story similar to the vague, half-dreamt imaginings of the professor. Peaslee goes to Australia, visits some ancient ruins, and finds the very volume he had written millions of years ago—when his mind was taken by aliens. Apparently his was not the only instance of intergalactic, temporal, "mind-napping":

> The essence was always the same—a person of keen thoughtfulness seized with a strange secondary life and leading for a greater or lesser period an utterly alien existence typified at first by vocal and bodily awkwardness, and later by a wholesale acquisition of scientific, historic, artistic, and anthropological knowledge: an acquisition carried on with feverish zeal and with a wholly abnormal absorptive power. Then a sudden return to rightful consciousness, intermittently plagued ever after with vague, unplaceable dreams suggesting fragments of some hideous memory elaborately blotted out.[17]

Such an anomaly enriches man's view of history, and helps to place him more accurately within the larger universe (and perhaps helps to explain the abundance of "mad" or "absent-minded" professors). But it has additional, sinister implications that Lovecraft tries to exploit to their fullest. There is a suggestion that incorporating self-knowledge of such magnitude will always be, by its very nature, monumentally frightening—a suggestion made by few writers working in this mode.

The third dominant mode of the incorporative variety is the class of SF stories that humorously depict the incorporation of some nondestructive element into the status quo. These stories make little attempt at plausibility, though they often incorporate scientific, "rational" explanations for the anomaly's acceptance. In L. Sprague deCamp's "Hyperpilosity" (*ASF*, April 1938), everyone on earth catches a virus that causes hair to grow in a fur-like covering all over the body. The protagonist desperately researches and finally discovers a cure for this virus and a way to remove everyone's excess hair. By that time, the population has grown to enjoy its new, biologically unprecedented development. The hair takes the place of clothing and becomes a source of pride and delight to many people. Unlike other modes of incorporative SF, this kind depicts a widespread, long-lasting, positive change, but is undercut by the nature of the change itself. The intent is finally humorous.

The incorporative variety of the subversive tale never really reached full fruition in the thirties pulps. The idea of projecting a full-scale utopia—or even of seriously depicting a positive "change" incorporated into society—did not, apparently, mesh smoothly with the dynamics of the pulp industry. The space allotted to single stories or installments in each issue of a magazine was brief, and most editors wanted a good part of each story to be filled with some traditional "pulpy" action. In the stories mentioned above, such action might be the discovery of a new plane of existence ("Upper Level Road"); the entrance into the lab of a monster from another dimension ("Vibratory"); or the struggle to discover a cure for a widespread virus ("Hyperpilosity"). Depicting social change usually requires much more space and nondramatic elements in the stories. Science fiction had to reach not only a generic but also a publishing-world maturity before the incorporative story could find a comfortable place in the science fiction canon. Most important, though, the seeds of it were planted in the 1930s SF magazines, and they were nourished for decades by some talented writers. That the incorporative story was carried into the next forty years of SF suggests that subsequent writers found the early, primitive versions of the formula to be influential and compelling, and that the vision this formula presented was one some portion of American society continued to view as important.

"THE PERSISTENCE OF VISION"

John Varley's "The Persistence of Vision," winner of the 1979 Hugo and Nebula Awards for best novella, represents a stage of development never reached by the subversive variety during the 1930s.[18] It brings together many paradigmatic features of the formula as outlined above, but does so in such a way that it exceeds the formula's usual constraints. These constraints—ones I have suggested were imposed by the pulp publishing industry—can be basically summed up as the necessity to make SF resemble other popular forms as much as possible. The status quo variety closely replicated the social affirmation found in most other pulp genres of the thirties. The subversive-destructive form often exploited the trappings and milieu that had come to be associated with SF by the mid-thirties: ray guns, space monsters, holocausts, destructive inventions, glamorous technologies, etc. While it did not stress such conventions, the subversive-incorporative variety deferred to the industry's constraints by working on a small scale; the idea that society needed large-scale improvement or overhaul was as inimical to the very conservative pulp magnates as it was difficult for SF writers to convincingly dramatize. In a sense, then, that the subversive-incorporative type of SF arose at all—even in a seminal form—is surprising. It is less surprising to see that this formula did not reach its fulfillment in the thirties; it did so only after the genre was accepted more thoroughly by the culture, and found expression in a number of different media. "The Persistence of Vision," a late 70s example of subversive SF, epitomizes the aesthetic possibilities of this form and, although the 30s varieties of this formula were inevitably less accomplished, Varley's story helps illuminate the durability of the formula.

The subversive form, as exemplified by "The Persistence of Vision," is ideally suited to blending science fiction with "mainstream" literature. There is a strong sense of naturalism in this story as well as what looks like an attempt at character development, something slightly unusual for science fiction until recently. It opens with an appropriately topical note: "It was the year of the fourth non-depression. I had recently joined the ranks of the unemployed. The president had told me that I had nothing to fear but fear itself."[19] Though the story is placed in what seems to be a near future, it is nonetheless firmly grounded in a readily recognizable status quo. In fact, it could almost be a 1930s Depression setting, complete with the FDR quotation. Varley mentions federal agencies such as HEW, the Department of Agriculture, the Bureau of Indian Affairs, and the like, fixing the space-time locale as one very close to our own. The narrator—who is never named—hitchhikes across the country, and while his adventures visiting communes and working for meals form the early portion of the narrative, they are mingled with the history and genesis of one commune he stumbles upon, "Keller," a place for the deaf, dumb, and blind offspring of a late 1960s rubella

epidemic. This early part of the story works at only a small remove
from a 70s status quo: it seems very like the average hitchhiker's
adventures. It is hardly displaced at all in time or experience.

Indeed, most of "Persistence" seems very unlike an SF story.
Its shape and structure actually subvert notions of what an SF
story should be: the narrator stays at Keller, learns the way of
life of these people, and becomes proficient—to an extent—in
their languages. This "everyday" quality to the story is what makes
it finally successful. The author so deftly and gradually subverts
a status quo reality that the anomaly he is employing does not seem
anomalous at all. Yet the idea of a group of over a hundred deaf
and dumb and blind people living in not just harmony, but communication so total that they could almost be considered to be
a single entity, is indeed anomalous. Each step the narrator takes
into the mysteries of Keller, the reader takes with him, however,
and the anomalous seems, therefore, commonplace. The narrator
describes his language experiences at Keller:

> As I became more fluent in handtalk, 'the scales fell from my
> eyes.' Daily, I would discover a new layer of meaning that
> had eluded me before; it was like peeling the skin of an
> onion to find a new skin beneath it. Each time I thought I
> was at the core, only to find that there was another layer
> I could not yet see. (p. 256)

The reader is in a similar situation: the anomaly at Keller reveals
itself bit by bit, in such a way that it seems a perfectly logical
progression from the previous step. It is an anomaly that not only
subverts the status quo of the story, but subverts reader expectation
as well: most readers probably expect a catastrophe to descend on
Keller, or possibly the revelation that Kellerites are aliens. Neither
happens. In fact, that "Persistence" is science fiction at all somehow
recedes into the background.

The initiation or education process the narrator undergoes at
Keller forms the largest portion of the story. The narrator first
learns the simplest form of language used in the commune: "handtalk." This involves forming the individual letters of a word into
another person's hand. Later he learns "shorthand," a form of
handtalk in which entire phrases can be expressed with one move-

ment in another's palm. Both types of communication are only slightly removed from what we know in our own world; the first actually exists, and the second seems an understandable development among a group of 115 blind-deaf-dumb people who live in isolation from the rest of the world. The third "layer of the onion" the narrator discovers is "bodytalk," a complex series of hand-body and body-body interactions, including sexual intercourse—which Varley uses as a metaphor for demonstrating how communication can take place through one's entire body—that reveals an enormously rich pattern of thought and expression. The whole body, here, is used as an instrument of communication. And grounding such a communicative form in a readily identifiable human act like sex makes "bodytalk" believable as a medium of exchange.

The later "layers of the onion" the narrator unpeels are more difficult to link to familiar experiences but, taken in context, they seem only slight extrapolations of the kinds of communication the narrator has already witnessed at Keller. "Touch" is difficult for him to describe, but involves the invention of a personal body language between each member of the commune and every other:

> It was a language of inventing languages. Everyone spoke their own dialect because everyone spoke with a different instrument: a different body and set of life-experiences. It was modified by everything. *It would not stand still.* They would sit at the Together and invent an entire body of Touch responses in a night; idiomatic, personal, totally naked in its honesty. And they used it only as a building block for the next night's language. (pp. 264-65)

"Touch," a language that proceeds logically from the other, intimate varieties, is a highly contexted, shorthand, personal version of bodytalk.

The final version of language the narrator encounters—and the one that makes him eventually leave Keller—has no name: it is represented by * * * or, in "Touch," three sharp slaps of the palm with fingers spread against the chest of another person. This is the "Touch" without touching, and only the original members of the commune (not, however, their children, who could hear and were sighted, and not, of course, the narrator) can practice it. It is an extension of "Touch" beyond physical boundaries, a group-practiced telepathic communication. This is a clearly anomalous biological ability, but a believable one in the context of the story. Though it is not one that is minutely described, Varley provides us with a familiar-world analogue. As the narrator sees people * * * ing, he relates, "The best analogy I could think of was the sensation a blind person might feel from the sun on a cloudy day" (p. 260). The narrator's sighted friend, a child of the original settlers named Pink, tells him more about it: "All I know for sure is that vision and hearing preclude or obscure it. I can make it as quiet and dark as I possible can and be aware of the edges of it, but the visual orientation of the mind persists" (p. 265). At this point the reader is so deeply imbedded in the layers of the onion and in the structure of the story, that the logic of * * * ing works. By having drawn the reader gradually and carefully into this anomalous world, Varley can show the utterly anomalous and bizarre in a comprehensible way.

Aside from the way its structure subverts common notions of how science fiction should work, "The Persistence of Vision" also employs traditional (that is, thirties) subversive SF tropes. It can, for example, be classified as the subversive-destructive variety, because the world as it is shown seems to be in the midst of a process of dissolution. Doom is impending in the world at large throughout the story, from the "fourth non-depression" opening to the self-destructing San Francisco closing. Other hints throughout the story suggest a dissolution, too: the roads and buildings are frequently in disrepair; urban violence—"the endlessly inventive street theatre"—is a commonplace; the country has already seen one disastrous meltdown of a nuclear plant.

"Persistence" rises above its predecessors in this mode, however, through its picture of the anomaly vis-à-vis the world's condition. The problem shown, Varley's picture of a dissolving society, is closely related to the anomaly. People in the outside world are totally absorbed in themselves, "their own way." What causes the world's problems—largely a lack of community—is the exact focus of the anomaly, Keller, which has attained an unheard-of, extraordinarily close-knit and cohesive community. Usually the destructive element, or the anomaly responsible for causing the disaster/dissolution, forms the focus in this kind of story, and often such a destructive element seems grossly out of touch with the status quo's faults. "Twilight," for all the majesty of its entropic vision, could well be seen as an overreaction to the industrial age, or worse, a picture that seems too far removed from everyday experience to have any applicability to the twentieth-century reader (in whose life, for example, "perfect" machines play virtually no part). Varley chooses not to dwell on the cause of social disintegration, but depicts instead a way to escape this status quo. And the escape route directly addresses the problems that have brought about the status quo's downfall.

"The Persistence of Vision" can be usefully seen as the in-corporative variety of subversive SF, too, because an agent of the status quo—the narrator—confronts and finally embraces Keller. Similar to the enclave variety of subversive-incorporative SF (such as "The Upper Level Road"), Varley's novella goes beyond the usual limits of this sub-genre in its elaborate treatment of the counterworld. The complex systems of lines etched in the walkways for the inhabitants to read with their feet, the way of dress, the sex mores, the personal relationships, and the history and language of the Kellerites are all carefully delineated in this novella. It seems as much an anthropological tract as a fiction. Linguistically, too, it recognizes the difficulty of a status quo-anomalous world confrontation; frequently the narrator resorts to dashes (to represent the untranslatable) or a series of paraphrases (to reflect the inability of words to adequately convey an expression in "body-talk"). In short, Varley projects a counterworld replete with the kinds of details 30s writers could not articulate, either because such details were too politically radical, or too explicitly sexual, or because they little resembled the action/adventure/cataclysm to be found throughout most of the pulps and most SF.

While "Persistence" is a tale of personal problem solving (like "Mind Over Matter" or "Vibratory"), it is also a *kuntslerroman,* a tale of an unsuccessful writer who travels to gain experience and develop as an artist. When Pink, the narrator's closest friend at Keller, asks him about his former life, he does not know what to say. His life had been that of "a permanently displaced person in a stainless-steel society" (p. 258). He is a picture of a 1970s man in trouble, a non-science fictional description of contemporary anomie. The narrator's stay at Keller solves many of his problems. He develops a close relationship with Pink, for example, and when he leaves the commune for a six-year stay in the world outside Keller, he is successful: "My writing came together and I sold" (p. 269). As part of his pattern of growth, change, and development, he returns to Keller near the story's conclusion. He has come to realize what things are important to him, and embraces them at the end in the form of Pink—and through her, the whole community. Success, material goods, and the part of the world perceptible through vision and hearing are all merely superficialities, which he rejects. The narrator represents and is the sole agent of the biologically "normal" world and the familiar social order, suggesting that this personal, artistic development he undergoes is one the rest of society could benefit from as well. Of course, it is unclear what exactly does happen at the end of the story: he returns to Keller, and suddenly loses his vision along with, presumably, his connection to the flawed outside world. How such a mystical transformation occurs is open to speculation.

The main reason the subversive variety of SF emerged from the thirties and flourishes today is that it offers a feasible way of recasting and subverting the conventional. The usual methods of subverting the status quo in SF are ones involving massive destruction or an eventual return to the usual that deny the actuality of any genuine threat to it. The subversive story provides not so much solutions to specific difficult situations as suggestions about alternative ways to address complex problems. What the incorporative mode does affirm is man's ability to finally solve the apparently insoluble. This type of SF demonstrates a faith in creative endeavor. Usually this faith implies exceeding the usual acceptable social boundaries: what may be a necessity as an ever-escalating, multifaceted doom seems settling in on late twentieth-century culture.

Finally, the most concrete thing offered by the subversive-incorporative form is a new mode of perception, anticipating the focus of the other world story. "The Persistence of Vision" refers not only to the tenacious way people with hearing and sight cling to a view of the world channeled through and dominated by these two senses, but also to the eventual fruition of a vision the blind-deaf woman has when she conceives the commune of Keller. She sees that she herself and people like her cannot live happy, useful lives in normal society, and that a communal situation like Keller could solve many of their problems. It is a new way of perceiving her situation. The reader, too, participates in a new level of perception. Change can be effected in this world, this story and others in the incorporative variety suggest, not only by actually altering the apparent reality, but by changing the way of perceiving things.

Though in part a product of the late 60s "love-peace" movement and the hippie counterculture, which relied so much on drugs to alter perception, "Persistence" also recalls its Depression era roots. The thirties were a time in which readers frequently had to call on personal resources after having been disappointed and defeated by the "system." Politically subversive, SF such as this suggests that in the absence of sustained political action, small-scale, personal, or internal changes should be attempted. Enough of them, added together, might conceivably change the larger world. Essentially, "Persistence" is a fiction that demonstrates a deep faith in man's basic goodness. If people were able to communicate utterly, with none of the distraction and equivocation of verbal communication, then harmony would be achieved. Of course, there is a sense of the womb-like in Keller, with its naked, sweaty, pansexual inhabitants groping among each other every evening after dinner. There is a desire, in the story, to return to the simple and the physical, to move away from the symbolic, the abstract, the complexity of modern society. Yet, just the same, "Persistence" suggests a possibility and metaphor for reform. By altering the most basic levels of human experience—perception and communication—the multifarious facets of contemporary social structures will eventually change as well.

NOTES

1. The endings of science fiction stories on film are apparently quite important to filmmakers. Consider the five endings to Jack Finney's novel, *The Body Snatchers* (1955). The book had two endings—one that appeared in its publication in *Collier's*, and one when it appeared as a book. The Don Siegel film (1956) also had two endings. The remake of the film by Philip Kaufman (1978) had yet another ending. For an excellent discussion of these many versions, see Glen M. Johnson, "'We'd

Fight. . . . We Had To': *The Body Snatchers* as Novel and Film," *Journal of Popular Culture,* 13, No. 1 (Summer 1979), 5-16.

2. L. Sprague deCamp, "The Blue Giraffe," *Astounding Science Fiction,* Aug. 1939, p. 114.

3. Arkady and Boris Strugatsky, "Spontaneous Reflex," in Isaac Asimov, ed., *Soviet Science Fiction* (New York: Collier, 1962), pp. 89-111.

4. Damon Knight, *The Futurians* (New York: John Day, 1977), p. 9.

5. Thomas Calvert McClary, "Rebirth," *Astounding Stories,* Feb. 1934, p. 131.

6. Arthur Conan Doyle, *The Poison Belt* (1913; rpt. New York: Berkley, 1966), pp. 98-99.

7. Donald Wandrei, "A Scientist Divides," *Astounding Stories,* Sept. 1934, p. 62.

8. Alva Rogers, *A Requiem for* Astounding (Chicago: Advent, 1964), p. 31.

9. Sam Moskowitz, *Seekers of Tomorrow* (1961; rpt. New York: Ballantine, 1967), pp. 51-52.

10. Don A. Stuart (pseud.), "Twilight," *Astounding Stories,* Nov. 1934, p. 48.

11. See Chapter 1, note 57, and the discussion of "Elimination" in Chapter 2.

12. Raymond Z. Gallun, "Mind Over Matter," *Astounding Stories,* Jan. 1935, p. 122.

13. Jack Williamson, "Born of the Sun," *Astounding Stories,* Mar. 1934, p. 38.

14. Warner Van Lorne (pseud.) "The Upper Level Road," *Astounding Stories,* Aug. 1935, p. 42.

15. Moskowitz, p. 380.

16. Lester del Rey, "Helen O'Loy," *Astounding Science Fiction,* Dec. 1938, p. 119.

17. H. P. Lovecraft, "The Shadow Out of Time," *Astounding Stories,* June 1936, p. 117.

18. The Hugo Award, named after Hugo Gernsback, honors the best science fiction that appears in a given year. The Nebula Award is similar except that science fiction writers (members of the Science Fiction Writers of America) choose the best works, rather than the "fans," as is the case with the Hugo.

19. John Varley, *The Persistence of Vision* (New York: Dial Press, 1978), p. 227. Subsequent references will be parenthetical.

4.
Other World Science Fiction

INTRODUCTION

Science fiction evolved as the thirties progressed, and the forms it took resembled less and less those found in other popular magazines. Science fiction began to differ from other popular fiction by showing situations in which no picture of standard social reality appears. If there is a connection to the outside world of the thirties, to the Depression, the bread lines, the international conflicts, the strife between labor and big business, it has to be inferred in much science fiction of the late thirties.

Such science fiction I label other world SF because it establishes a fictive universe that works on principles entirely different from those of any naturalistic world. Such principles may be as diverse as those underlying an entirely matriarchal world or those of a world in which men have been replaced by machines. They can include pictures of earth in the far future ruled by insects, or earth of the distant past when Neanderthal man competed with Cro-Magnon man. In short, this form of science fiction focuses on worlds that are patently nonexistent.

Of course, a certain number of connections are made in such stories with the so-called "outside world." The pattern of action closely resembles something that is happening outside: two distant planets could be shown warring over a small body that is between them, for example; or extremely intelligent, futuristic insects could be shown organized into a social structure that resembles a communist state. The connection these stories make with specific social events must, however, be inferred. There are invariably some forces or characters in every story that the reader is able to identify; there are also numerous forces that seem quite alien and only metaphorically connected to the world of the reader. Such a dichotomy inevitably causes conflict within each story: the communalistic bugs are usurped by a "plucky" individual; the two primitive, warring planets could both be overcome by a third faction which uses weapons of pure energy and is an example of a future superstate that is unconcerned with petty territoriality.

The task for the science fiction critic is to discover what, in these stories that apparently have no relation to familiar thirties reality, are specific references to that reality, and what is completely projection. In essence, the critical task starts with identifying the familiar element and continues by assessing the conflict between this familiar element and the bulk of the story.

The principal focus in the other world story, and that which must form the basis for any serious discussion of the text, is a genuinely alien consciousness or culture. Much of the story will be devoted to developing such an agent in the other world, demonstrating how different it is from the known and the familiar. Whether it be an insect mind, or an alien that is constantly hungering after food, or a society's obsession with an ordered, rational way of life, this alien consciousness is the focal point of the story. Any hint of the surrounding twentieth-century milieu would appear as a deviation from the alternative world.

The other world's response to the anomalous element—to, that is, some reality familiar to the reader—resembles the response made by status quo reality to the anomaly that appears in stories of the status quo or subversive type. The other world either rejects or is subverted by the agent of recognizable times and values. This real world agent might be an earthman visiting another planet, or an atavistic impulse on the part of some other world inhabitant. The earthman can, for example, be killed or ousted, or he can subvert the values of the planet he is visiting. The atavistic impulse can be quashed by the other world, or it can form the vanguard for a new, revolutionary movement.

By "borrowing" the two main structures of science fiction—the status quo and the subversive structures—the other world story can usurp the reader's notions not only about surrounding social reality, but also about how science fiction helps to interpret that reality. This brand of SF stresses the "alien's" point of view to such an extent that in a successful story, that point of view finally becomes one the reader is able to share. Any recognizable, real world element introduced into the alien world is at once stripped of its usual milieu and cast in a new role. The utility of the New Deal, for example, is dramatized effectively in "Intra-Planetary" (*AS,* October 1935) by Nat Schachner. This story chronicles events in the life of Tubo, a "protoplasmic form." Tubo travels from planet to planet before coming to the realization that he should not "blindly and without thought spawn innumerable progeny" because then, "the planets cool and we in our folly with them."[1] Tubo instead proposes "Birth Control, a new deal! . . . It had such a satisfying, mouth-filling sound" (p. 60). He concludes that "the new deal must go on, even though we as individuals die" (p. 61). The world of Tubo disappears toward the end of the story, as it is revealed that Tubo himself is merely a cell in the body of a cancer patient receiving some miracle serum. The plight of Tubo, which involves traveling in a murky void in hopes of finding food and shelter, is quite convincing: it is a recognizable, understandable, real world activity. The reader is swayed by Tubo's argument for conservation of natural resources, for limiting a population in the face of dwindling supplies and foodstuffs. Indeed, even when it is shown that Tubo is one cell in a human body, the arguments he makes do not lose their cogency. The overall argument of "Intra-Planetary," too, is strikingly dramatized; cast in other-worldly terms, the view of the New Deal as a mere survival measure in a cancer-ridden body politic seems to carry some weight.

Like much other world SF, "Intra-Planetary" uses a metaphorical situation to bridge the gap between popular and "serious" literature. A number of stories in this formula are more firmly fixed within popular literature formulas. Indeed, other world SF represents a curious mixture of popular fiction conventions with those of more serious literature. It is this brand of science fiction that represents the most mature variety of the genre, the most imaginative, ingenious, and, finally, the most serious form of science fiction today. That the two major science fiction forms of the thirties helped produce it suggests that science fiction as a genre was beginning to draw upon precedents that were not wholly derivative from other popular forms, but were ones that science fiction writers and readers had themselves helped to establish.

THE FLAWED OTHER WORLD STORY

The type of other world formula most closely related to usual science fiction forms is the "flawed" other world formula, which begins with the picture of a strange, alien world. The drama of the story is that this world comes into conflict with and succumbs to recognizable, traditional, twentieth-century values. This form is so similar to other science fiction, and probably arose in the thirties, because it is yet another variety of SF in which the familiar reality of the reader is shown triumphing over the strange. The pattern this formula takes can be diagrammed as follows:

Other World ——► Some facet of ————► A vs. R ——► The Triumph
(Anomaly, A)   Reality, R   of Reality
                            (A representation of
                            contemporary or human
                            values)

As usual, the conflict is between the known world and some future version of it, or between the known world and some bizarre, entirely projected, fantastic realm. But in this version, the agent of the depicted status quo has to have even more energy and effectuality than it had in the status quo formula. In the flawed other world form, "R" has to do more than fight off invasion or remain stable when faced with some invention or unusual happenstance; it has to have the vitality to triumph over a world in which the anomalous predominates.

Edmond Hamilton's story, "The Island of Unreason," is a paradigmatic example of the flawed other world story. First published in *Wonder Stories* in May, 1933, and recipient of the Jules Verne Award,[2] "Island" has been widely anthologized since, and still holds interest for today's reader. Hamilton himself has gone on to become a major science fiction writer and has published a wide variety of science fiction and fantasy tales. It is not surprising that he is one of the originators of a spin-off of the usual status quo pulp science fiction story.

Like most flawed other world stories, "The Island of Unreason" opens with the picture of a world that could be considered an extended, distorted variety of our own. That is, the removal from typical status quo reality is not very great: "The Director of City 72, North American Division 16, looked up enquiringly from his desk at his assistant," the story opens. It deals with men and women, to begin with, in contrast to, say, some alien creatures, and North America still exists. Even the specific locale is almost recognizable as part of the industrial sprawl of the thirties: "He looked . . . at the big office, at the keyboards of the big calculating and predicting machines, at the televisor disks through which could be seen cities half around the world, and at the broad windows that looked out across the huge cubical metal buildings of City 72."[3] Though the profusion of numbers and machines suggests a very different world, it is one not too far removed from the realistic one of the thirties and one that appears in other fiction of the decade; it is a world within reach, but something has gone wrong with it to produce a dehumanizing landscape.

The story opens with the sentencing of a "criminal," Allan Mann, who has been charged with breach of reason:

> The specific charge is that Allan Mann, who has been working two years on development of a new atomic motor, refused to turn over his work to Michael Russ, Serial number 1877R6, when ordered to do so by a superior. He could give no reasonable cause for his refusal but stated only that he had developed the new motor for two years and wanted to finish it himself. As this was a plain breach of reason, officers were called. (p. 971)

Clearly the "breach of reason" has some close relation to assembly-line production, which, though more efficient than techniques involving single-worker craftsmanship, is less satisfying to the individual worker. "I had worked on the motor so long I wanted very much to finish it myself, even though it took longer," Mann explains to the authorities. Confronted with a strangely impersonal world, the reader, like Mann, identifies with values that come from the twentieth century. Lest the reader overlook the connection being made, Hamilton has the Director of City 72 explain to Mann: "Reason has brought us up from the barbarism of the twentieth century and to commit a breach of reason has become a serious crime" (p. 971). The face-off here is between a future world with its own set of "reasonable" and efficient organizational principles, and a twentieth-century man (his name is clearly suggestive) who instinctively questions these principles.

The surviving feature of the barbaric twentieth century here is "unreason," one that is linked with images of creativity, vitality, and excitement. Mann is transported to the "Island of Unreason," the place where all "unreasonables" are sent. Though he has repented before going, his is the penitence of a child before an angry parent, Hamilton suggests: Mann still has faith that he will be provided with "bed and food and hygienic amusements . . . by a paternal government" (p. 972). In short, he still has faith in the government, and feels that he has made a mistake for which he is being justly and "reasonably" punished. The fictive strategy, of course, involves keeping Mann an agent of the alternative world as long as possible so that his interaction with the agents of twentieth-century-like "unreasonables" will be interesting and filled with conflict.

And this Island of Unreason, over which the Directors do not preside, is replete with adventure. The first person Mann sees is "a girl clad in a stained, ragged tunic." Her attire and demeanor are those of a savage: "Her black hair was cut very short, and as she threw herself back from him in alarm a short spear in her right hand flashed up ready to dart toward him" (p. 973). After assuaging her fear, Allan explains his plight. She understands immediately, and remarks, "Those fogies of directors send someone here every few days or so." Clearly this is a counterworld that has some attractions, not the least of which are rebellious, scantily-clad women.

There would not be enough conflict if Allan were immediately won over to the side of the unreasonable. Instead, he is offended at this woman's "heretical description of the executives of the reasonable world," and tries to personally maintain the standards of "reason" on this prison-island. The conflict between the agents of the other world and those of the known, recognizable reality forms the bulk of the story in this formula, as it does elsewhere throughout SF. Allan only gradually learns to sleep and survive in the wilds, to fight another man to protect his woman, to eat meat, to feel the languor that follows physical exertion. These are actions he at first detests, but then grows to enjoy greatly. Although living in the wilds is not an exact duplication of 1930s social reality, it is nonetheless far closer to thirties lifestyle than is the social system of the powers-that-be. On this island people can mate with whomever they choose ("When people mate there's no Eugenic Board to assign them to each other'' [p. 973], the girl explains); they eat foods that are closely derivative of living matter (rather than the "mushy predigested foods" provided by the authorities); they can even perform religious ceremonies. "We've a religious preacher here that was sent here because religion's unreasonable too" (p. 977), the girl explains to Allan. Finally, the Island of Unreason offers Allan Mann not only adventure and excitement, but a higher morality as well.

The conclusion of "Island of Unreason" suggests a victory of thirties values over those of this future parent-world. Rather than rising up against the parent-world, Allan Mann embraces the values of those on the Island, and rejects the establishment and all its insistence on the orderly and the "reasonable." Since Allan, once a thoroughly indoctrinated citizen in City 72, is completely won over to the Island's way of life, then any man, the story suggests, is likely to be won over. Like many stories in this mode, "Island" ends not with an actual takeover of the establishment by the small group of people representing thirties values, but with a promise and a hope that this group—which is clearly superior to the other-world faction—will someday rise up and ascend to power: ·

> "Some day," said Hara, "when there's a lot more of us unreasonables we'll go back there and take the world and make it all unreasonable and inefficient and human again."
> "Some day—"Allan murmured. (p. 977)

Like much science fiction of the thirties, "The Island of Unreason" questions the future of the technological society, and shows that the way twentieth-century society is headed may point toward dehumanization, loss of individuality, and the like, but that sane, "human," contemporary values will struggle against this trend.

VARIATIONS AND AESTHETIC POSSIBILITIES

The basic fictive strategy of the flawed other world formula is to show human existence and consciousness against a backdrop of other possible existences and all possible consciousnesses. Rather than bolstering common contemporary values, as does the status quo form, or subverting such values, as does the subversive form, this type of other world formula lets contemporary values and ideas struggle within totally alien situations. The anomalous is granted ascendancy over the conventional from the outset. An odd, often striking light is shed on the known and the familiar. Irrationality and disorder, for example, supplant an ordered, mechanistic world in "The Island of Unreason," a situation made more complex since much of modern society and thirties society seem to be striving for an ordered world. The tension in all versions of this formula, though, centers around the agent of contemporary reality. How this agent or representative of the known responds to the pressure of the bizarre generally provides a comment on contemporary values.

One interesting feature of the formula is that the comment on contemporary reality is made through a picture of the alien and the bizarre. Each story starts out by showing an "other" world, and this world is apparently the focus of the story. It is usually internally consistent, and seems quite removed from contemporary reality. But as the story progresses, this other world is shown to be flawed and gives way to some recognizable problem or situation. The focus then shifts away from the other world to the recognizably familiar. The picture of the other world actually forms a kind of lens through which the familiar world is viewed, and it is this lens that SF writers most often experiment with to achieve unusual and interesting pictures of the known world.

The other world is often, for example, shown to be an absolute reification of the dreams of contemporary reality. "The Island of Unreason" follows this strategy, giving a picture of a world that is well-ordered, free from crime and disharmony, and able to provide for all its inhabitants. But this story is not as effective as it might be because Hamilton presents the other world from the very beginning as flawed and sterile. People have numbers instead of names. The main character is denied his very understandable desire to finish a project he has worked on for years. In the more accomplished versions of this formula (like Lawrence Manning's "The Elixir" [*WS*, August 1933]), the other world is attractive for a time—man's dreams seem realized therein. Manning's story opens on a world—in A.D. 25,000—privy to the secret of eternal youth. Into this highly attractive atmosphere, into this world that seems to be utopia itself, an element is introduced that recalls the world of the reader. A twentieth-century man wants to know the "reason or purpose of existence."[4] At first, this "old fashioned" element is seen as threatening and unpleasant, but later, as the story draws to a conclusion, the reality-agent is shown to have effected positive changes in the other world. The twentieth-century man establishes "Temples of Thought" in this future world to examine the meaning of life. The reader is thereby brought through two distinct emotional stages: he is first attracted to the other world, and as the contemporary values strive to usurp it, the reader logically sides against these elements, which seem to be undercutting the "dream." But gradually, these undercutting social elements prove themselves to be better than the reified dreams.

"Rex" (*AS*, June 1934) by Harl Vincent, for example, begins with a picture of the ideal robot operating in a world full of robots that serve man:

> It was a thing of glistening levers and bell cranks, of flexible shafting, cams, and delicate mechanical fingers, of vacuum tubes and photoelectric cells, of relays that clicked in ordered sequence when called upon to perform their myriad functions of pumps, tanks, condensers, reactances, microphones, and loudspeakers. A robot, created by the master scientists of the twenty-third century.
>
> . . . this robot was the chief of the mechanicals; its control tubes and relays provided the ability not only to diagnose swifty and unerringly the slightest electrical or mechanical faults of the lesser robots but to supervise their correction.[5]

This is Rex, the master robot surgeon, and he is the supreme creation of twenty-third-century science. He is more properly an android than a robot, inasmuch as he looks like a man ("the marvelous mechanisms were housed in a body like a Greek God's"); and indeed his judgment is considered so reliable that men do not even have to oversee him as he operates. He is, in sum, "man's most perfect servant," the culmination of this robot-dependent future society's know-how.

The wondrousness of this robot and the world he operates in diminishes, though, as the story progresses. Rex is a little too perfect: he begins to reason on his own and decides it would be best for him to actually control the robots and for the men to start to work again. At first, this seems quite unfortunate. Well-fed, comfortable, housed, catered-to, humans of this age live a pleasant, even sybaritic existence. And the alternative to this existence that Rex has in store seems horrible: he plans to breed a new race of beings using the physical superiority of robots linked with the mental and emotional capacity of humans. Such a blend will be effected through eugenic breeding, surgery, experimentation, and—the real-world thirties element—a return to hard work by the men themselves. "Many tasks were beyond the strength of men whose muscles had softened from disuse and dissolute living," but Rex's program of work for ten hours every day toughens up the populace. As the story develops, it seems that Rex is a necessary catalyst for this world; his presence is cutting out the flab in this future society. That he is so easily able to undermine the social order suggests that such an order is somehow flawed, too.

Eventually Rex is successful in the experiments he designs to give himself emotion, and he kills himself out of rage and frustration. Perfect machines, it appears, cannot abide the powerful irrationality of human emotion. Another recognizable human element— emotion—similar to the "unreason" in Hamilton's story, demonstrates its strength over and antagonism to a mechanical, ordered robot. The country is soon returned to normal through "hard work by the scientists." "But a thought that lingered faintly in the minds of several of them was voiced by Innes, when he said: 'I—I'm almost sorry. In one way, it was a great opportunity. . . .'" Indeed, there is an ambivalence to the story that is nicely conveyed; though Rex is partially monstrous in his ambitions, the fact that people begin to work once more in an attempt to create a better race suggests that his motives are not entirely ill-conceived. The order he seeks to establish must have had a certain appeal to thirties audiences.

Another fictive strategy taken by writers of the flawed other world formula involved showing the other world as enormously, antithetically different from familiar thirties reality, and then inserting into this very removed world a facet of the known and the familiar. Lee Gregor's story, "Heavy Planet" (*ASF*, August 1939), initially conveys an impressive sense of difference from the usual and familiar:

> The little craft . . . took a leap into the air and seemed to float for many seconds before burying its keel again in the sea. It often floated for long distances, the air was so dense. The boundary between air and water was sometimes scarcely defined at all—one merged into the other imperceptibly. The pressure did strange things.[6]

Not only is the atmosphere unfamiliar on this planet, but the inhabitants are far from human-like as well. When an earth-based spaceship arrives on Heavyplanet, the main character, Ennis, boards it by opening a hole in the hull: "The rent was too small; he enlarged it by taking the two edges in his hands and pulling them apart. As he went down he looked askance at the insignificant plates and beams that were like tissue paper on his world" (p. 35). Just to assure the reader that this is an earth-vessel, Ennis is shown examining the charts in the control room. The main chart is of a solar system with nine planets. Human-scale materials— the steel of a spaceship—are like cardboard to Heavyplanet's enormously powerful inhabitants.

Ennis is looking for something that the earth vehicle could provide: some facet of human technology that is not flimsy and slight on this different world:

> —and there it was. He recognized it at once. It was big, squat, strong. The metal was soft, but it was thick enough even to stand solidly under the enormous pull of this world. He had never seen anything quite like it. It was full of coils, magnets, and devices of strange shapes to him. . . . It was atomic energy. (p. 35)

Immediately realizing he has to save this power source from the hands of other nations on the planet, Ennis goes about fighting off approaching battleships. At the story's climax he holds this atomic powered blaster in his hands and fires it at the opposing forces, completely obliterating them. Atomic energy, even on this planet of superhumans, is a frightful and powerful weapon—highly useful to them. No longer would the "race of men on Heavyplanet [be] doomed to stay down on the surface of the planet, chained there immovably by the crushing gravity" (p. 35).

By showing the dream of atomic energy—a theme that had received a multitude of treatments by the late thirties—having such an effect on the inhabitants of a planet so different from earth, Gregor is able to cast an odd, interesting light on this dream. First, atomic energy is shown as something of awesome power, able to disrupt the balance of power on a planet where the environment has created beings who are awesomely strong in their own right. Second, the question is raised of the utility of atomic weaponry to relatively weak races like humankind: suppose the weapon had fallen into the hands of one of the two forces opposing Ennis on Heavyplanet—both of whom are warlike and "would use it against all the other worlds that abounded in the universe" (p. 35)? Finally, by employing such a structure, Gregor is able to create a metaphor: atomic energy in our world would have an effect similar to what it will have on Heavyplanet. We, too, once we have mastered this new power, will no longer be chained to our earth—of conventional values and ideas—and many new aspects of the universe will be open to us as well. Inasmuch as the story was written in 1939, it is easy to make the connection between the warring nations on Heavyplanet and the many warring nations on earth. In short, by removing the locale of atomic strife to a remote planet, Gregor is able to comment on one feature of the known world that received much attention in science fiction but which was seldom dramatized so convincingly: the impending danger of atomic weapons. Though atomic power is shown to have liberating aspects, its introduction into a flawed other world can also cause havoc. Introduction of it into our own world would also bring dangers as well as rewards.

Another variation on the flawed other world formula is demonstrated in John W. Campbell's "Tharoo" story, "Rebellion."[7] The initial other world is that created by the Tharoo, who have dominated earth and humanity for three thousand years. The first story in the series, "The Machine," shows mankind dependent on a vast machine for its livelihood. The machine withdraws its support toward the end of that story, and mankind faces a very different kind of lifestyle. The second story in the series, "The Invaders," describes the invasion of the Tharoo, a race looking for a new planet, and their successful methods of enslaving humanity to make the world a better place for both mankind and the Tharoo. Both of these stories follow a flawed other world pattern, each introducing the real-world notion of "work" into a world in which people do not have to work, in which either a machine or an abundant planet provides them with sustenance. "Rebellion" opens with the assumption that mankind has finally relearned how to work and produce. The only unfortunate thing about the race's position now is that the Tharoo are mankind's masters and oversee every aspect of life, from mating to invention.

In "Rebellion" the feature of twentieth-century man introduced into the initial other world is one that is ordinarily thought to be negative: deception. Some highly trusted human eugenicists secretly breed a race of man that has extraordinary powers. This superior human race routinely falsifies records and keeps itself hidden from the Tharoo until it is more intelligent and powerful than the Tharoo themselves. There is a positive sense, once the Tharoo are ousted, that mankind is now finally on its own, and therefore superior to what it had been under the domination of the Tharoo. But this positive sense is blemished because mankind has had to reacquire a basically negative trait—rebelliousness, and with it, secrecy, cunning, lying, and the like. To be sure, mankind's capacity for deception is what eventually overcomes the invaders, but now that refound capacity has to be lived with.

Campbell's stories were often provocative, and often gave interesting insights on apparently worn-out science fiction themes. Invasion from another planet was a theme that found its way into probably 75 percent of the science fiction stories written between 1930 and 1939; yet in the "Tharoo" stories, it has a freshness to it. By using the flawed other world structure, Campbell is able to inject new life into an old theme.

Atomic power is another well-worn topic of science fiction stories; thirties writers exhausted almost every possible situation that the development of atomic power could generate even before its actual discovery. Campbell, however, employs the flawed other world formula in "Atomic Power" (*AS*, December 1934), and achieves an odd, interesting effect. He uses atomic power not so much as a symbol for incredibly powerful weaponry or, for that matter, as a commentary on the power inherent in the atom, but as a device that helps him demonstrate man's place in the universe.

"Atomic Power" opens with a picture of an other world in which atomic power is commonplace. The engineer at the opening is "boredly smiling" as he explains an atomic power plant to some students. It is revealed that virtually all of the world's power comes from the atom, and that a major portion of their environment is "a great maze of subsurface tunnels."[8] The atomic power plant runs on water, breaking down the oxygen and hydrogen to create energy. As the students look on, a drop of water gets stuck in the machine, refusing to break down. "No one understands why," the engineer explains; it is "just that the generators stop abruptly and cannot be restarted till they are cleared of the charge contained" (p. 88). They used to examine these drops that would not break down, the engineer recounts, but they found that was too costly. Such drops are now merely discarded.

With no apparent transition, Campbell then depicts a fairly conventional real-world situation, involving "Ban" Torrence, "a physicist to the core," and "Tad" Albrite, "engineer," two contemporary hero-types complete down to the nicknames in inverted commas. Ban and Tad observe some small but disturbing changes in the earth's physical laws, and attempt to right things before these changes magnify and destroy the world. This story within a story follows the more or less traditional status quo pattern, in which the heroes attempt to compensate for and thrust out some anomalous, threatening element. Indeed, Tad and Ban are successful—and just at the last minute, too—because they are able to see man's place in the larger universe. Tad explains:

> —I think that Earth and the solar system—[are] just an atom in a greater universe. But they're releasing atomic energy in that greater universe—and we're the atom! If my theory's right, then I can release atomic energy myself and stop their release of *our* energy by just slightly upsetting their field, so that it passes by, harmless. Not a terrific amount of energy needed. The field would spread out from this apparatus here—if it would work—at the speed of light. (p. 96)

Indeed, the invention does work, but only on the second try. The first drop of water Tad tries to break down for some reason refuses to disintegrate. Apparently there are worlds within worlds within worlds. The structure Campbell uses for this story dramatizes not only this idea but also the general insignificance of our own world when it is viewed against the cosmic order, an order in which it is only a very small part. The other world that opens the story "Atomic Power" can affect our world very substantially without its ever being aware of our existence. To survive, therefore, our world must reshape its view of the universe. Though it is a story of our world's alteration in the face of anomalous circumstances (which include the destruction of buildings, and the widespread breakdown of atomic structures), it is also a story that places the known world in a large, overarching system of universes. The other world of the opening is flawed only insofar as it cannot destroy every single drop of water in its atomic generators. Research, hard work, invention, and insight on some atom-sized world within the drop are the ways the other world's apparent flaw can be sustained.

Another sub-type of the flawed other world story also places humanity and the known world in a large perspective. Stories of prehistoric times show how certain human traits became important, and how the older forms of man were selected out. This larger view, unlike the cosmic, expansive one offered by "Atomic Power," is historical and evolutionary. "B.C. 20,000" (*AS*, April 1932) by Captain S. P. Meek, and Lester del Rey's "The Day Is Done" (*ASF,* May 1939) are both stories of prehistoric intrigue, and both follow the flawed other world structure. Del Rey and Meek both start from the other world of precivilized man—the Neanderthal man struggling against Cro-Magnon man, to be specific—and then inject some element of recognizable modern values into their tales. Del Rey shows the last Neanderthal's world as the flawed other. The contemporary is suggested by the culture of Cro-Magnon man as it impinges on the inferior one of the Neanderthal. Such traits as oral communication, group living, and weapon production are those that seem anomalous to this last Neanderthal, and eventually his own lack of such "survival skills" causes his death. The story, told from this "last man's" point of view, dramatizes what it is like to be usurped by a stronger, more adaptive race, and the sadness that accompanies such a displacement. S. P. Meek, on the other hand, starts with the early form of Cro-Magnon culture as the flawed other. Men struggle over women, and weaken their own tribe through such internal conflict. The element of our world introduced into this intrigue-ridden prehistoric culture is, finally, monogamy: it is shown to have some survival value. Both of these stories use the flawed other world structure to make the reader sympathize with the problems faced by our own supposed ancestors. They conclude by showing that modern customs and trends stemmed from prehistoric roots, and that all evolutionary progress came about as the result of an anomaly's being introduced into a flawed other world. Unlike previous forms of science fiction, this subvariation diminishes or bolsters contemporary values only insofar as it offers an evolutionary rationale for given social institutions, such as marriage, and given behavior patterns, such as weapon production.

This formula often shows the "other" in such a way that real-world elements seem genuinely alien and threatening when they are introduced. "The Island of Unreason," for example, in no way fleshes out the alternative world; even the main character, Allan Mann, is quickly won over to the "barbarian" lifestyle once he has spent a short time on the island. "Rex" comes a little closer, showing human society as being very pleasant since the dawn of the labor-saving robots. When a ten-hour-a-day work routine intervenes, it seems at first a painful routine for this culture. Yet the reader soon realizes that it is a therapeutic one. "The Day Is Done," on the other hand, portrays the plight of Hwoogh, the last Neanderthal, as genuinely sad throughout; even as he goes through his final few days being humiliated by the superior race (who resemble modern man), his point of view is the sympathetic one:

> Hwoogh's old friends had come back to him in his dreams, visiting him and showing the hunting grounds of his youth. He had heard the grunts and grumblings of the girls of his race, and they were awaiting him. The world was still empty of the Talkers, where a man could do great things and make his own kills, without hearing the laughter of the Cro-Magnons. Hwoogh sighed softly. He was tired, too tired to care what happened.[9]

The better examples of this kind of formula produce an ambiguous effect, diverting some of the sympathy the reader might ordinarily feel for his own kind toward the alternative life form or culture. The best examples of this formula actually make the reader perceive through an alien consciousness.

In general, though, this type of story attempts to be more than simply disorienting. A majority of these stories are politically reactionary, suggesting that there are better, perhaps more "natural" times to which man should return. "The Island of Unreason," for example, suggests that society's movement into a rigidly ordered bureaucracy ought not to overshadow the valuable things in life like adventure, sexual choice, and religion. "Rex" and "The Machine" have similar implications, portraying as empty and shortsighted the dream of a world filled with mechanical, work-saving devices. Nat Schachner's "The Orb of Probability" (*AS*, June 1934), through a picture of a world in which "everything was predigested, prearranged, precalculated for [men] by the omni-present machines,"[10] epitomizes the formula's reactionary impulse. The "heroes" of this future culture invent a machine that re-institutes "chance" or "probability," and they are transported back to New York City of the twentieth century. Chance has it that "time had gone haywire" (p. 133). Here, they hope to "bring back the old spirit of adventure, of struggle with nature that was so satisfying" (p. 133). The "orb" self-destructs, and these in-habitants of A.D. 9678 are permanently fixed in the twentieth century. By introducing a standard feature of the familiar, contemporary world into stories about supertechnological futures, the future world is deflated, while the known, common world emerges as exciting by comparison.

Finally, this flawed other form conveys a sense that there is some value in adversity. Most of these stories focus on facets of the known and familiar that are often unpleasant or restrictive: work, monogamy, contingency. Yet they suggest to their readers that there are pleasant and delightful things imbedded in even the most mundane chores. Without these twentieth-century obligations, which make for some difficulty in living one's life, the world would be a lusterless place. Moreover, many of these stories suggest that these quotidian tasks and social strictures form the very foundations of our culture's strength. Without work, we would regress into a decadent and dissolute race. Without monogamy, society would be torn with internal strife. Without chance, all would be dullness. This flawed other world structure is ideally suited to compensating for possible discontent among its audience. It shows the least pleasant aspects of everyday life to have a value that extends well beyond the everyday, and imbues mundane duties with a sense of variety and worth.

THE ASCENDENT OTHER WORLD STORY

One common type of other world science fiction story in the thirties undercut a major popular literary convention by showing conventional, earthly reality as inferior by contrast with an other world. The "ascendent" other world formula starts from a base-level anomaly; it opens on an other world only remotely connected to our own. Unlike the opening of the flawed other world form, which generally implies a connection to present-day reality, the ascendent other world opening often takes place on a planet or in a dimension different from earth in kind, rather than simply in degree. Instead of opening on an other world, say, which is a future extension or prehistoric interpolation of human history, the ascendent other form opens with an "other" that has clearly gone far beyond conventional values and social structures. And the portion of recognizable reality introduced into the other world, expectedly, has little hope of changing that world. Though the agent of contemporary reality generates some conflict, it is a conflict whose outcome is inevitably going to sway against the recognizable, against the known. Humankind is squashed, bug-like, at the conclusion. The pattern this formula follows can be diagrammed as follows:

Other World ——▶ Some facet of ——▶ A vs. R ——▶ Other World
    (A)   contemporary   (conflict)   prevails
               Reality (R)

Generally this story pattern addresses the eclipse of the known by the unknown, or shows the feebleness of the familiar when it is backgrounded against the very different.

Leslie F. Stone's story, "The Conquest of Gola" (*WS*, April

1931), is an excellent example of the ascendent other world story pattern. One of the few stories written by a woman that appeared in the SF magazines of the thirties, it has as its subject the relationship between men and women in society. The other world it presents is on Venus (known in this story as "Gola" by its natives), on which women are the supreme beings, and "sweet gentle males" are kept as consorts. Besides depicting an "inverted" social arrangement, Stone presents aliens who have a weird biology. The suggestion, too, is that such biologies are superior to human ones: "Our fine circular bodies . . . our beautiful golden curls, our power to scent, hear, and touch with any part of the body . . ."[11] Clearly this is not an advanced state of humankind. If anything, the natives represent an extension of myths about the feminine body, personality, and eroticism in general. Humanity's interaction with them will almost inevitably be antagonistic.

The agent of contemporary reality that impinges on this other world is often viewed through the perception of the alien beings. Filtered through such an alien lens, this picture is generally negative, demeaning. The "Matriarch" of Gola explains the social organization of "Detaxal" (earth):

> On Detaxal it is different, for there the peoples, the ignoble male creatures, breed for physical prowess, leaving the development of their sciences, their philosophies, and the contemplation of the abstract to a chosen few. The greater part of the race fares forth to conquer, to lay waste, to struggle and fight as the animals do over a morsel of worthless territory. Of course we can see why they desired Gola with all its treasures, but we can thank Providence and ourselves that they did not succeed in "commercializing" us as they have the remainder of the universe with their ignoble Federation. (pp. 1279-80)

Assuredly this is an earth that has advanced somewhat over the culture of the 1930s from which the story emerged. Yet it has recognizable features of contemporary reality. The division of labor into classes that separate the abstract and scientific thinkers from the masses, the seemingly instinctual aggressiveness, and the desire to commercialize, are all features common to twentieth-

century American civilization, all features that will strike home to
the contemporary reader.

The conflict between these two story elements—the other world
agents and these agents of contemporary reality—usually is a somewhat one-sided affair. The other world is so superior a foe that
mankind as we know it stands little chance against it. In "The
Conquest of Gola," for example, the inhabitants of Gola assume
that the men who have arrived must have had their spaceships
built by their mothers. Throughout, the natives are unable to
take seriously the overtures of the earthmen, because on Gola,
men are "ineffectual weaklings," "gentle and fun-loving."

Such a story would be very brief if there were absolutely no
contest at all between our world and the other. Therefore writers
working in this formula show the agents of known reality making
extraordinary, near-superhuman attempts to overcome the ascendent
other. In "The Conquest of Gola," for example, the men construct
a radio device to contact earth; they insinuate themselves into the
bedchambers of their Golan women captors, and stir up the males
of the planet to insurrection. There is even a hint that the earthmen
might sexually intimidate the Golan females. As one earthman,
Jon, ties up the narrator on the eve of the insurrection, she remarks,
"How strong he was! For the moment a new emotion swept me,
for the first time I knew the pleasure to be had in the arms of
a strong man . . ." (p. 1286). But such clever scheming and planning is for naught. The radio does work (more earth ships arrive);
the males of Gola do revolt; and the Golan women do develop
a slight affection for the earthmen. Earthmen even take over the
city—for a time—"establishing already their autocratic bureaus
wherever they pleased" (p. 1287). But the Golan women tele-
pathically hypnotize the men, and the invaders are destroyed.
The formula usually works by showing mankind valiantly struggling
against desperate odds—a common enough situation in popular
fiction—but losing.

The conclusion of this kind of story suggests that, like the
Golan males, our male-dominated society is weak. Here, as elsewhere in the formula, such a criticism is more overriding than
specific; these stories do not, as a rule, define areas of weakness,
or make any suggestions for improvement. The flawed other
world pattern would often suggest such areas, whether they be
mankind's overdependence on machines, or his desire for atomic

weaponry. The ascendent form, by contrast, denigrates the entire social organization familiar to readers. It shows mankind in conflict with something so alien and superior that catastrophic changes in contemporary society, technology, or biology would be needed for man to match up fairly to this alienness.

Other stories in this mode do not show man (and specifically, men) in such a demeaning way. Rather they attempt to place civilization as we know it in some larger schema. But unlike flawed other world stories that accomplish a similar end (like Campbell's "Atomic Power"), the ascendent other form shows our world as a passive element in a grand design. This form, taking the long, evolutionary/entropic perspective, often depicts the world of the far future, when mankind has been "selected out," or when entropic forces have reduced human civilization to rubble.

Two stories following such a pattern are "The Last Men" (*AS,* August 1934) and "Green Glory" (*AS,* January 1935), both by Frank Belknap Long. Long's own description of them is accurate. They are "scientifantasies of the far future, when the ants and other insects . . . had taken over, enslaving the whole of mankind and reducing men and women to tiny creatures only a few inches in height."[12] The strategy in these stories involves showing how the very small, impotent men and women are entirely subservient to the insects' wishes. One goes slightly against the insects' advice in "The Last Men," and picks a physically beautiful mate. Both he and his mate are destroyed. In "Green Glory," the human hero, Atasmas, sacrifices himself to the cause of the ants in the war between the aphids and the ants. The queen tells Atasmas when the latter has volunteered for the death mission: "In your humble way you have the sublime, selfless mind of an insect."[13] The humans display all the usual popular literature traits of the thirties; the couple in "The Last Men" are desperately in love: "The woman in his arms was unbelievably beautiful: she lay limply and calmly in his embrace, her eyes luminous with tenderness."[14] Atasmas, similarly, is courageous and inventive. At one point he is saved by a beautiful woman with whom he falls in love. But both he and the woman are sacrificed to the death mission against the aphids. There is no hope for even dauntless and romantic men and women rising up and reconquering this other world. Mankind's dominion has passed long, long ago.

Stories that effectively dramatize how human civilization will be subject to entropic forces often take the ascendent other form. Robert Moore Williams's story, "Robot's Return" (*ASF*, September 1938), shows the return of robots to a desolate and uninhabited earth. They possess consciousness and a sense of history, though, and attempt to discover what form preceded them: "The future is built of material taken from the past," one of the robots remarks, "and how can we build securely when we do not know what our past has been?"[15] They eventually discover a fallen statue with an inscription which explains that mankind was wiped out by a bacteriophage. In the midst of the bacterium's attack, a scientist sent off a rocket full of humans in suspended animation, and accompanied by several robots. Apparently, the robots are the only ones to survive. "Rust" (*ASF*, October 1939), a similar story by Joseph E. Kelleam, depicts the struggles of three surviving robots on a planet that has long been uninhabited. The robots had been designed to be engines of war, and they clumsily attempt to repair themselves, using their unsuitable mechanical appendages: "We were not fashioned to make anything," one remarks, "only to kill."[16] There had been some mixup during a global conflict and all the robots on the planet killed all the men. Now the mechanical, even sentient, weapons roam the planet, and slowly disintegrate as a result of the ravages of the elements. At the story's conclusion, the last robot is himself buried beneath an ever-growing pile of snow; the machine's last act is, significantly, to destroy a statue of a child. Mankind was inventive enough to implant his wisdom and consciousness in a housing more permanent than human flesh. But in the end the machine eventually crumbles, too, subject to natural processes. Kelleam's story implies that mankind's foolish destructiveness aids the ineluctable working of entropy. But both stories suggest, more than anything else, that all elements of recognizable, contemporary society, as well as human civilization, are merely temporary, overshadowed by the larger rules of the universe.

The emphasis in the ascendent other world story is on the perception of the surrounding universe. All of these stories ask, that is, how contemporary reality will be viewed against the larger backdrop of future history, or against the wider context that alien cultures can provide. And the emphasis centers, finally, on those facets of society that will have lasting value, or on those

features of humankind that, while existent today, will be seen in the
future as quintessentially human. The two Long stories, for
example, ask what human traits will still exist when mankind is
small and weak by comparison with the insects. Williams and
Kelleam raise perhaps an even more interesting question;
although their stories deal with sentient robots, they are robots
programmed by men, and through their programming, something
of humanity remains. "Robot's Return" and "Rust" speculate on
what is of lasting value when men no longer exist in physical
form on the planet, and man's only legacy is the programs that
the machines follow.

The major aesthetic challenge facing the writer of ascendent
other world stories is making the world he creates simultaneously
very different from known reality and comprehensible to the
reader. Many stories, for example, err by creating a world that is
simply too far removed from the conventional, one that is too
bizarre and anomalous. Few stories of this sort appeared in the
thirties SF magazines, though; if anything, the majority of SF that
appeared in them was not removed enough from contemporary
reality.

But Clark Ashton Smith's story, "The Demon of the Flower"
(*AS*, December 1933), appeared in *Astounding*'s early thirties transition period, and was so dense, complex, and removed from
any allegorical or direct picture of human and recognizable reality,
that it is almost incomprehensible today.[17] It is a story that discusses the inhabitants of the planet "Lophai," a world inhabited
by motile, communicating plants. "Alive and restless," these
plants struggle among themselves. One wants to rebel against
the supreme plant, the "Voorqual," and seeks the aid of a rival
plant, the "Occlith." Yet once the rebellion is successful, the
perpetrator's betrothed turns into a reincarnation of Voorqual,
"to preside forever above the city Lospar and the world Lophai."[18]
Though an ambitious story, "The Demon of the Flower" is finally
a little too removed to be interesting. It is difficult to sustain any
concern for a plant world that has no human element. The one
lesson that it teaches may be that human intrigue and cunning
are of no use in alien cultures, but such a lesson is not, finally,
made to appear particularly important or relevant to the—
assuredly human—reader.

RECENT EXAMPLES AND NEW DEVELOPMENTS

Moderan (1971), a contemporary novel by David R. Bunch, is similarly removed from experience. Though intriguing in its creation of a world where humanity survives in the "flesh-strips" left on cyborg-like creatures, it is finally too bizarre, too much the "other." Even the language attempts to reflect the alienness, the lack of humanity of Moderan (ellipses are the author's):

> The cords all in scattered snarls and little tangle-ball heaps now . . . the shredded paper torn hastily, frantically from and in its own wild piles now . . . The room a shambles, but THE DREAM there cool . . . the blonde doll all turned on, the real and true copied image of an old Dream in my mind . . . there waiting in the body that science had made, the little bow of a mouth all moist and rosy-red, the blue eyes blue-bulb blue and like small glass globes sliced carefully out of that heaven when June was all clear-and-bright . . . and now here to look at me like two sweet queen from paradise, light and language and love-bespeaking-love for this empress come visiting from heaven . . . no more than a body's length away . . . SO I MOVED INTO THAT MOMENT . . . snatching away what was necessary to snatch away of her clothes . . . my heart on MAX entirely now, hers on LOVE ME COOL . . . factory set. . . .[19]

Though *Moderan* has been highly praised by science fiction critics, it is nonetheless difficult and tedious to sustain an interest in this other world for 240 pages. The "lesson" of *Moderan*—impending eco-disaster, loss of humanity, anomie and plasticization of modern life—is learned in just a few pages, and little amplified by the various episodes the hero goes through.

More successful tales of this type generally make an explicit link to the contemporary reality of their authors, and give a sense of the other world without actually subjecting the reader to the alienation such a culture would cause. Thus Ursula LeGuin, in *The Left Hand of Darkness* (1969)—a novel about a planet, Gethen, on which the inhabitants can become either male or female during the mating period every month—chooses to use the pronoun "he" throughout (in reference to the natives) so as not to distance the reader too much from the experience of the novel. There are constant reminders that the Gethenians are "ambisexual," but such reminders are imbedded in the body of the text rather than in the language. Inventing a new pronoun, or using "he/she" or some variety of it throughout, would have stood as a barrier to communication, would have been intrusive.

The ascendent other formula is well adapted to expressing a general disaffection with modern life that a great deal of contemporary literature and art reflects. There are things flawed with our own world and with our culture, this formula suggests, and it is a historical inevitability that our world will be superseded. One contemporary version of the ascendent other story, Thomas Disch's "Fun With Your New Head" (1970), exemplifies how this type of science fiction can create a sense of the hideously different but still be readily comprehensible to the reader. Yet, curiously, this picture, like many others in the ascendent other formula today, is basically disconnected from any notions of historical process: the author does not make it clear how our culture will progress to the future state he depicts.

Disch's story concerns a culture that uses parts of other cultures' flora and fauna for decoration and amusement. Human heads are one such collectible, imported by "Exo-Imports, Inc." The entire story takes the form of an advertisement for the HEADS:

> HEADS are so funny. Listen to the limbless talking HEAD talk about "Freedom," "Death," "Beauty," and "God-Father." Make the HEAD fall in "Love" with you. Any HEAD can be made to "Love," if training manual instructions are carefully observed. Watch the worn-out HEAD die, talking, talking, talking till the moment it decays. Indeed, it is not an exaggeration to say HEADS are so funny. . . .
>
> Many designers consider HEADS to be an attractive addition to the decor of one's environment, especially in arragements with contrasting xeno-flora and xeno-fauna. For the fashion-conscious HEADS are available now in a range of natural

tints from brown through pink. When treated with new, special formula *Fungi-X*, HEADS can also be cultivated in more agreeable colours, though fungifying processes will abbreviate markedly the life-time of the HEADS so treated.[20]

Although this trivialized picture of mankind presented by Disch is shocking, the formula itself suggests that mankind is going to be somehow subordinate in the other world, and therefore stories such as Disch's very pessimistic one are only logical extensions of the formula. There is a hint, too, in this story, that mankind has a similar relationship to other, subordinate cultures, taking their most cherished icons and features, commercializing them, and finally making them trivial. It is never explained in the story if the "bioengineering. . . practised by the wild-four-limbed progenitors and manufacturers of the HEADS" is only an advertising ploy. It may be, that is, that this culture is merely capturing and modifying humans. Or, perhaps worse, humanity artificially creates these life forms for export. In either event, contemporary values like love, or talking, or, for that matter, heads attached to bodies, have been ignored in order to satisfy the demands of intergalactic commercialism. The story stresses most strongly the subordination of contemporary values to those of an alien superrace, rather than any full-fledged historical process—a view it could easily have presented, considering the dramatic situation and overtones.

In contrast to Long's thirties stories, which show mankind subjugated by the insects, "Fun With Your New Head" does not soften its impact by suggesting that humanity will eventually, some day, end up as trivial and unimportant, but implies that mankind as it exists today is subject to such trivialization. In fact, there are similarities between what the alien culture of "Exo-Imports, Inc." does and what twentieth-century civilized man does. Disch's story finally suggests that the relationship among very different cultures or species is often a flawed one, and that the superior faction will always tend to demean the inferior ones. Just as modern man has no compunctions about using animals as decoration or as amusements, or cherished icons of primitive cultures as ornaments, so cultures vastly surperior to our own will not hesitate to amuse themselves with our senses, our emotions, and even our heads.

A literary tack thirties writers seldom took, but which the ascendent other form implies, also bypasses views of history. Some SF shows human biology as being repulsive when backgrounded against that of the alien culture. "The Conquest of Gola" suggests that man (and men) is alien, but never was this suggestion stressed as much as it is in the contemporary science fiction stories of Stanislaw Lem and other writers.[21] One excellent example of the possible display of humanity as repulsive is found in a story by the French writer J. P. Andrevon, "Observation of Quadragnes" (1971).[22] It is a simple story, taking the form of a diary that an alien keeps as he observes two human beings he has captured and caged for study. The two people, an American man and an Italian woman, are alone and naked in a small room, and unable to either communicate or escape. Not surprisingly, they spend a great deal of time copulating. The alien's description of their sex practices makes such functions indeed sound bizarre, and removes from them any trace of the erotic. The suggestion, in fact, is that they are ludicrous, and even a bit repulsive:

> Finally, Quadragne A introduced his ventral tube (which in the meantime achieved its maximum length) into the small vertical cleft which Quadragne B possesses beneath her posterior parts, concealed under a hairy surface and through which she ordinarily discharges her liquid excrements. Quadragne A, holding his victim firmly upright, then began to jerk up and down in place, with the effect (of course I was observing the process with a powerful magnifying lens) of slipping his ventral tube into the interior of the cavity of Quadragne B. The back and forth movement achieved an accelerated rhythm, and the two Quadragnes began to moan softly. (p. 70)

Though there is of course an element of the absurd to this description, there is also a sense that the description is accurate, and that the alien is right. The most attractive things may also appear, from a different perspective, as repulsive: the story nicely captures the attraction/repulsion of sexual activity.

An even more interesting development of this type of science fiction is that evidenced by some of Stanislaw Lem's tales in *The Star*

Diaries (1971). In the "Eighth Voyage," all of human history and achievement is shown to be flawed and deplorable. Again, a similar stress was suggested by Leslie F. Stone's "The Conquest of Gola," in which the earthmen are emblematic of the things that are wrong with human civilization: they are warlike, exploitative, chauvinistic, entrepreneurial. Lem, however, makes the picture of a flawed earth civilization much more explicit. Ijon Tichy, earth diplomat, is sent to the "General Assembly of the United Planets," in an effort to help have earth admitted to the Assembly. He meets a creature—a "Rhohch"—who is to plead earth's cause before this august body of other-worldly creatures. Before the meeting of the General Assembly, this creature has to be briefed by Tichy on earth history. The Rhohch asks Tichy of earth's great achievements:

"Atomic energy, one may assume, you already have at your disposal?"

"Oh yes! Yes!" I eagerly assured him.

"Marvelous. But wait, ah, I have it right here, the head-chairman left me his notes, but his handwriting, h'm, well . . . and for how long have you availed yourself of this energy?"

"Since the sixth of August, 1945!"

"Excellent. What was it? The first power plant?"

"No," I replied, feeling myself blush, "the first atomic bomb. It destroyed Hiroshima. . . ."

"Hiroshima? A Meteor?"

"Not a meteor . . . A city."

"A city . . .?" he said, uneasy. "In that case, h'm, how to put it . . ." he thought for a moment. "No, it's best to say nothing," he decided. . . .

"Try to recall, any grand feat of engineering, architecture on the cosmic scale, gravitational solar-launchers, well?" he prompted.

"Yes . . . that is, work is under way," I said. "Government funds are rather limited, most of it goes into defense . . ."

"Defense of what? The continents? Against meteors, earthquakes?"

"No, not that kind of defense . . . armaments, armies . . ."

"What is that, a hobby?"

"Not a hobby . . . internal conflicts," I muttered.

"This is no recommendation!" he said with obvious distaste. "Really, you didn't come flying here straight out of the cave!"[23]

Again, the overtones are humorous, but the general thrust of the section is a serious one: how would earth's history look to an outsider? The possibility of depicting the history of civilization on this planet in any way other than negatively seems, Lem tells us, almost impossible.

The phase of the ascendent other form in which humankind valiantly struggles against the alien is bypassed altogether in recent enactments of the formula. It is precisely those actions which in the thirties would form the focus for some action sequences that are lampooned in these examples. Romantic love can be programmed into the human HEAD in Disch's story; it is grotesquely detailed in Andrevon's "Observation." And the classic struggle between earth creatures and the alien inhabitants of other planets is shortcircuited in the Lem piece: Tichy (whose name translates as "hush" or "quiet") finds himself involved in a debate (not a heroic battle) with an alien, and it is a debate he has not the least chance of winning.

The formulas which came out of American science fiction magazines of the 1930s have now been absorbed not only by modern science fiction, but into foreign cultures as well. The formulas of science fiction eventually have come to transcend their own historical milieu. SF has become a kind of fiction that is able to address mankind's problems, able to make statements about all of mankind without restricting itself to one culture. Though Lem's story seems to imply a criticism of Western culture— specifically of its use of the atom bomb—and Andrevon may be criticizing the lack of originality of Americans, and Disch (an Englishman) is certainly making a judgment against American advertising and commercialism, all these stories attempt to be statements about the status of civilization as a whole. In reference to "The Conquest of Gola," Hugo Gernsback remarked in 1931:

> Americans are fond of ridiculing the customs, habits, and temperaments of people of other nations. Similarly other nations pick our peculiarities as a source of amusement. We all think that what we do, think, or say is natural and inevitable, and that the actions of others are "queer."
>
> Similarly, if we were to travel to a strange world, and find different forms of intelligent life, we would be mon-

strosities to those people, as much as they would be to us. We would find it more difficult than we imagine to even establish the most elementary form of communication, because our mental processes would have practically nothing in common.[24]

Science fiction has become a forum for looking at those things humanity has in common, and noting how they would appear against the background of all possible imaginative projections of them.

One reason a formula such as the ascendent other emerged is that, finally, it is a type of fiction that dramatizes powerlessness. It has become very apparent in this century, as man has developed all sorts of technological advancements that help him adapt to society, that such advancements are not really entirely conducive to a better life. The dream of a better world probably gathered momentum as obvious changes in man's physical surroundings came about—the widespread use of electricity, the internal combustion engine, synthetics, and the like. This dream was undercut not only by the Depression of the 1930s, but even more by the introduction of atomic energy and the continuation of global conflict for many years after World War II. The ascendent other form of science fiction suggests that powerlessness is inevitable, and that human history is flawed. If man is to be superseded, these stories suggest, then it is because he is basically maladaptive, bestial, and bellicose.

NOTES

1. Chan Corbett (pseud.), "Intra-Planetary," *Astounding Stories,* Oct. 1935, p. 58.

2. Ashley remarks: "In these pre-Hugo award days, a spasmodic Jules Verne Award was given to popular stories." Michael Ashley, *A History of the Science Fiction Magazine, Vol. I: 1926-1935* (1974; rpt. Chicago: Regnery, 1976), p. 154.

3. Edmond Hamilton, "The Island of Unreason," *Wonder Stories,* May 1933, p. 971.

4. Laurence Manning, "The Elixir," *Wonder Stories,* Aug. 1933, p. 158.

5. Harl Vincent (pseud.), "Rex," *Astounding Stories,* June 1934, p. 143. The distinction between "android" and "robot" is true only in English. In *R.U.R.* by Karel Capek (Czechoslovakia, 1922), the artificial creations were human-looking, but called robots. Apparently the word robot is derived from Czech. *robic,* to work, or from *robotnik,* serf.

6. Lee Gregor (pseud.), "Heavy Planet," *Astounding Science Fiction,* Aug. 1939, p. 34.

7. All the "Tharoo" stories were published under the Don A. Stuart byline: "The Machine," Feb. 1935; "The Invaders," June 1935; and "Rebellion," Aug. 1935.

8. Don A. Stuart (pseud.), "Atomic Power," *Astounding Stories,* Dec. 1934, p. 88.

9. Lester del Rey, "Day is Done," *Astounding Science Fiction,* May 1939, pp. 49-50.

10. Nat Schachner, "Orb of Probability," *Astounding Stories,* June 1935, p. 111.

11. Leslie F. Stone (pseud.), "The Conquest of Gola," *Wonder Stories,* Apr. 1931, p. 1282.

12. Frank Belknap Long, *The Early Long: The Hounds of Tindalos* (New York: Jove Books, 1978), p. 22.

13. Frank Belknap Long, "Green Glory," *Astounding Stories,* Jan. 1935, p. 46.

14. Frank Belknap Long, "The Last Men," *Astounding Stories,* Aug. 1934, p. 59.

15. Robert Moore Williams, "Robot's Return," *Astounding Science Fiction,* Sept. 1938, p. 142.

16. Joseph E. Kelleam, "Rust," *Astounding Science Fiction,* Oct. 1939, p. 136.

17. When *Astounding* was taken over by Street and Smith (and its editorship by F. Orlin Tremaine) in late 1933, it initially printed fantasy stories rather than science fiction. See Leland Sapiro, "The Mystic Renaissance: F. Orlin Tremaine's *Astounding Stories,*" *Riverside Quarterly* 2 (June 1966), 75-88; 2 (Nov. 1966), 156-70; 2 (Mar. 1967), 270-83.

18. Clark Ashton Smith, "The Demon of the Flower," *Astounding Stories,* Dec. 1933, p. 138.

19. David Bunch, *Moderan* (New York: Avon, 1971), p. 61.

20. Thomas Disch, "Fun With Your New Head," in *Under Compulsion* (1970; rpt. London: Granada, 1978), pp. 128-29.

21. See Stanislaw Lem, "Prince Ferrix and Princess Crystal," in *The Cyberiad* (New York: Avon, 1976), pp. 227-36.

22. J. P. Andrevon, "Observation of Quadragnes," in Franz Rotten-

steiner, ed., *View From Another Shore* (New York: Seabury, 1973), pp. 61-83.

23. Stanislaw Lem, "The Eighth Voyage," in *Star Diaries* (New York; Avon, 1978), pp. 25-26.

24. Hugo Gernsback, editorial blurb introducing "The Conquest of Gola" in *Wonder Stories,* Mar. 1931, p. 1280.

5.
Conclusion

In general, what I have attempted in the foregoing pages has been a formula-analysis of 1930s science fiction. This early period of SF production was characterized by fairly simple, unadorned plots, language, and characterization which laid bare the writers' narrative strategies. Although contemporary SF is apparently more complex and certainly more spectacular, it can be usefully analyzed by comparison with its antecedents from the 1930s. Most of today's science fiction writers were first SF fans, and were weaned on just the kind of literature published in the thirties; it is not surprising that their writing is linked to thirties SF in structural ways. This resemblance between thirties and contemporary SF is significant when coupled with the knowledge that the thirties was the first decade in which science fiction reached a large audience, because it can then be posited that the thirties witnessed SF's emergence as a distinctive genre. One major limitation of this study is that it fails to trace the evolution of science fiction between 1940 and 1975, and by this omission may seem to imply that there was no evolution at all, only a constant and considerable outpouring of SF stories in the three basic formulas articulated by thirties SF writers. In fact, though, the genre has developed enormously over this interim period, and has grown into a multifaceted mode of narrative that pervades the media and arts: but that evolution is the subject for another study.

Formula-analysis of science fiction has the advantage of clearly placing the genre within the ambit of the popular literature critic. Future studies could more closely relate science fiction to detective, western, adventure, romance, and even—as I implied in my analysis of *Alien*—to pornographic fiction. This series of links with other popular genres has only been suggested here, and clearly warrants more precise formulation. Most popular genres rely on a conventional pattern of action; most allow for considerable reader identification with one or more of the characters; most employ straightforward, idiomatic (as opposed to literary) language; most have a distinctive type of protagonist (the "hardboiled" detective; the taciturn, low-key cowboy; the naif of romance or pornography); all have so firm a place in the culture that the images and conflicts they summon could be considered archetypal. Science fiction is unique in its capacity to subsume many of these genres and in its ability to displace the familiar and unchanging conventional world so much popular fiction assumes. It is necessary, however, to admit that SF is a kind of popular fiction, too, and that its popularity is a result of many of the same sociocultural factors that generate interest in other kinds of popular fiction.

Viewing science fiction as another manifestation of popular culture and consciousness enables the critic to reclaim much of the literature that has been passed over. Stanislaw Lem and Darko Suvin, for example, hold that 95 percent of all science fiction is unworthy of critical attention. Perhaps such a figure implies more than anything else that it is impossible to read and critically evaluate more than 5 percent of this genre anymore. The popular culture critic, however, can be somewhat less parochial in his scope, can analyze and draw from the "condemned majority" of apparently transient literature, and can discover the ways its structures and conventions inform the "elite 5 percent." After all, this 5 percent would probably not have been produced without the supporting scaffolding that the more routine SF provides.

Examining the broadest range of SF, including that which is commonly dismissed as formulaic, the critic finds that the genre as a whole does not obey rules of scientific accuracy and plausibility. Most science fiction stories are not scientifically accurate or even plausible when viewed by the scientific expert. And a smaller portion of the condemned 95 percent bears resemblance to actual scientific possibilities than does literature from the top 5 percent, perhaps because this elite category of SF is aimed not only at the more literary but also at the generally more sophisticated reader who is abreast of intellectual trends and developments in many fields.

Some of the stories discussed herein clearly have a scientific angle—Schachner's "The 100th Generation" speculates about eugenic experimentation; Burks's "Manape the Mighty" about interspecies brain transplants; Van Vogt's "Black Destroyer" about the anthropological link between culture history and behavior; Belknap Long's "The Last Man" about the possibilities of future evolution; Wandrei's "A Scientist Divides" about the evil potential of protoplasm experimentation. All these scientifically-oriented themes have special relevance today, when recombinant DNA experiments are a reality and General Electric is (as I write) attempting to patent a new life form. Yet the science in science fiction should not, I am suggesting, be taken as defining the genre: it is only a verification device which allows the author to convincingly present his or her idea of the social mechanism. Its small claim to actual "scientificality" and its usual ignorance of the facts and complexities that real science deals with allow the story to be a corridor into what often seems an inaccessible, hermetically sealed discipline, but one that has—for better or for worse—great impact on large numbers of people. SF offers this apparent entry into a given field, and demystifies its concepts and ambiguities. That these demystifications are often scientifically naive or wrong is finally of little moment: for the value of the story, in the methodology I have proposed, inheres in the way it speculates about social adaptations to anomalous circumstances, not in its scientific accuracy. Stories about robots, for instance, are not serious cybernetic extrapolations or speculations; stories about inventions of new elements (such as "The Ultimate Metal" by Nat Schachner) are not serious scientific assessments of how molecular structure can be alchemically transformed. Rather, the scientific angle is used as a point of departure for some consideration of social processes.

By establishing common ground among multiple themes, this formula methodology implies that future work in the field would do well to look more closely at the underlying similarities and not so much at the surface variety of SF. "Theme" criticism is now widely practiced, of course, and this is not to say that it is not valid. Rather, I mean to encourage those critics with little knowledge of science to approach the genre: it is not literature that may only be evaluated by scientists or futurists.

One other possibility this methodology implies is the examination of science fiction before 1930. What was premodern SF like? Poe, Melville, Twain, Hawthorne, and Verne wrote science fiction-like pieces that could be usefully interpreted through formula-analysis. Though generally the anomalous element is less dominant in these stories than in modern SF, it is nonetheless unmistakably present. Much of this SF would probably obey the status quo formula, but it would be interesting to see what kinds of emphases and variations of it are to be found in pre-twentieth-century SF. The social/publishing world circumstances that at once spawned and limited the development of such a form are also worthy of closer investigation.

Further thought and research are needed as well to properly apply formula-analysis to both more lengthy and more complex literary constructions. Recent SF novels are especially difficult to anatomize using this technique, largely because they usually employ more than one formula. In fact, the overall structure is often contrived to sustain a number of different, self-contained (but often integrated) formulas. Though a SF novel will frequently prolong a section of one formula—say, the anomaly-reality conflict—or string one formula after another onto its narrative thread, a type of SF, metafictional SF, is becoming increasingly popular, and can be less readily classified or parsed. Metafictional science fiction focuses on the fiction-making process itself and almost always calls into question what "reality" is in a story, how much is "anomaly," and how much is simply the author's invention or speculation about what he or she could invent. The point of such a narrative strategy is often that the recognizable and nonfamiliar repeatedly blur. Routinely, in these stories, the anomaly is only an idea in the protagonist's mind, a lurking and powerful creature of his/her personal, subjective universe. In such cases, the formula-methodology clearly requires another level of sophistication so that it may more readily be used to accommodate characterization and ambiguity.

The connections between the formulas and the surrounding culture that produces them are extremely important, and very difficult to define. If science fiction is more socially than scientifically dynamic, the social influences on it should probably be thoroughly articulated. The social, political, and cultural history that I bring to bear on the fiction is only of the most general sort. Attempting to make more explicit connections between the fiction and the world outside it—the thirties—would prove a difficult, many-layered task. I still believe, however, that it is not an impossible task, that through the use of fan histories, the study of media from the thirties—newspapers, magazines, radio shows, movies, catalogs, best-sellers—and the study of thirties art, an overall sense of the decade can be acquired. Perhaps the general history I have applied has worked well enough to warrant the application of a more specific history. On the other hand, its apparent success here may be a function of its generality: future work in the area would do well to assess how close a correspondence can be usefully made between popular fiction and the milieu that produced it.

The critical terminology offered in this study is preliminary rather than final. To say that one major element of the SF story is a depiction of "reality" oversimplifies and misstates the function of even popular art. Calling one component of a story "reality-depiction" implies that experience is somehow transcribable, or that literature itself is a simulacrum of life. Clearly, no matter how vivid or lively words on a page are, they offer only a very abridged version of reality or life experience. The model they suggest, or the picture they render, will always be incomplete and selective. The science fiction writer is doomed, though, not only to making inadequate and incomplete renderings of the phenomenal world— as are all artists—but also to forever trying to portray anomalous elements through the use of conventional language. How can the inhabitants of Flatland ever appreciate three dimensions when all they have ever known are breadth and length? This issue is not a great problem when dealing with the mass of more ordinary thirties science fiction, but it is one that any critic of contemporary SF must meet head-on. SF is at once related to and subversive of the phenomenal world. It is at once referential and nonreferential. It renders a certain view of experience as well as a certain model of possible experience. As the methods and concerns of science fiction become more assimilated by mainstream writers (Thomas Pynchon, John Barth, Robert Coover, Stanley Elkin, Gilbert Sorrentino, and Jorge Luis Borges are some examples), and genre-SF becomes more complex, the two basic elements of 30s SF become more difficult to locate, label, and analyze.

The most successful and convincing emphasis in this study is on science fiction as a literature of change. As I read through hundreds of thirties science fiction stories, I was struck again and again by the superficiality of the science and the lame justifications for introducing "anomalous" circumstances, yet the enormous amount of authorial energy demonstrating how society reacts to the anomaly. It is almost as if the anomaly's existence were an accepted premise; the fictive task is then to exploit the possibilities of this premise rather than to question its scientific underpinnings. The SF of the era implied, therefore, that change happens to people rather than happening within them. The picture that this fiction suggests is of marionette-like people, less interested in who controls the strings or why they are made to do certain things, than in how an unprecedented play of the strings will shape tomorrow's routine. The focus is not on the instilling, say, of knowledge, or on the development of social/personal/political possibility. Instead, SF depicts individuals adapting to sudden, drastic, media-transmissable change—which is, in a society in which information has become more important than knowledge, a well-known form of change. It is in no way surprising that people are very interested in the surgical operations, superfuels, and H-bombs that, with the flick of a dial, could suddenly become overwhelmingly important features of their lives. Science fiction is an understandable expression of a society in which world views can change as rapidly as technology.

The commentary that SF makes on such change can be inferred from the formula-analysis I have suggested. The status quo variety implies that such changes do indeed happen and cause excitement, but are finally not threatening to society's integrity. The subversive form is less optimistic and lends a greater efficacy to the anomalous: society can—and often should—be disrupted by a new element introduced into it. The other world formula suggests that such a dynamic is operative in circumstances so removed that elements of the contemporary world are themselves the anomalies: the structure of the other world story asserts that radical, widespread, media-transmissable change could happen in other cultures than our own, and is in fact an underlying feature of all social organization.

Another pleasant discovery I made along the way was that much of today's SF is very similar to that produced in the 30s. The proportions of formulas are different than they were in SF's formative decade—today there are many fewer status quo and considerably more other world stories—but the same basic patterns still inform much of the genre. A corollary of this, that many of the stories I have recovered and examined are of high quality, is also true: the stories of Nat Schachner, Raymond Z. Gallun, John Russell Fearn, Stanton A. Coblentz, Donald Wandrei, and Leslie F. Stone are intelligent and entertaining, and deserve to be made accessible to today's vast SF audience.

It is unusual that a type of literature can be embraced by a popular reading audience, complex enough for the literary critic to study, and rich enough for the serious fiction writer to borrow from. And it is clear that this type of fiction will have continued relevance in a society characterized by rapid change and information overload, and its further study and practice will help, in numerous ways, to illuminate that society.

Appendix: Fiction from *Astounding Stories/ Science Fiction,* 1930-1939

An asterisk indicates that the story has been discussed or mentioned in the text.

Asimov, Isaac. "Trends." July, 1939.

Auckland, Roi. "Blind Reasoning." Feb., 1934.

Ayre, Thornton (pseud. of John Russell Fearn). "Penal World." Oct., 1937.*

_____. "Whispering Satellite." Jan., 1938.

Barnes, Dave (pseud. of Arthur K. Barnes). "The House That Walked." Sept., 1936.

Bates, Harry. "A Matter of Size." Apr., 1935. See also: Anthony Gilmore, A. R. Holmes, and H. G. Winter (pseudonyms).

_____. "Alas, All Thinking!" June, 1935.

Beaumont, David H. "When the Cycle Met." Nov., 1935.

Beckett, William C. "Duel in the Space Lanes." Mar., 1938.

Berryman, John. "Space Rating." Oct., 1939.

_____. "Special Flight." May, 1939.

Binder, Eando (pseud. of Otto Binder). "The Anti-Weapon." Feb., 1938.

_____. "Eye of the Past." Mar., 1938.

_____. "Life Disinherited." Mar., 1937.*

_____. "Orestes Revolts." Oct., 1938.*

_____. "Queen of the Skies." Nov., 1937.

_____. "Rope Trick." Apr., 1939.

_____. "Set Your Course by the Stars." May, 1935.

_____. "Ships That Came Back." Nov., 1935.

_____. "S.O.S. in Space." Jan., 1937.

_____. "Spawn of Eternal Thought." 2 pts. Apr.-May, 1936.

_____. "Strange Vision." May, 1937.

_____. "The Time Contractor." Dec., 1937.

_____. "The Time Entity." Oct., 1936.

_____. "When the Sun Went Out." Sept., 1937.

Boch, Oscar A. "Spacewreck." Nov., 1939

Bond, Nelson S. "Down the Dimensions." Apr., 1937.

_____. "The Einstein Inshoot." Nov., 1938.

_____. "Lightship, Ho!", July, 1939.

_____. "Stowaway." Aug., 1939.

Bowman, B. L. "Laboratory Co-Operator 3." Jan., 1936.

Breuer, Miles J. "The Einstein See-Saw." Apr., 1932.

_____. "A Problem in Communication." Sept., 1930.

Buchanan, Carl, and Dr. Arch Carr. "Discus Men of Ekta." Feb., 1935.

_____. "Warriors of Eternity." Aug., 1934.

Burks, Arthur J. "Done in Oil." June, 1939.

_____. *Earth the Marauder.* 3 pts. July-Sept., 1930.

_____. "The Fatal Quadrant." Feb., 1938.

_____. "The First Shall Be Last." Jan., 1939.

_____. "Follow the Bouncing Ball." Mar., 1939.

_____. "The Golden Horseshoe." Nov., 1937.

_____. "Hell Ship." Aug., 1938.

_____. "Jason Sows Again." 2 pts. Mar.-Apr., 1938.

_____. "Lords of the Stratosphere." Mar., 1933.

_____. "Manape the Mighty." June, 1931.*

_____. "The Mind Master." 2 pts. Jan.-Feb., 1932.

_____. "Monsters of Moyen." Apr., 1930.

_____. "My Lady of the Tunnel." Nov., 1933.

_____. "The Trapper." Sept., 1938.

Campbell, Clyde Crane (pseud. of Horace L. Gold). "Age." Apr., 1935.

_____. "The Avatar." July, 1935.

_____. "Fog." June, 1935.

_____. "Gold." Jan., 1935.

_____. "Inflexure." Oct., 1934.

Campbell, John W. *The Mightiest Machine.* 5 pts. Dec., 1934-Apr., 1935. See also: Don A. Stuart and Karl Van Campen (pseudonyms).

Carr, Dr. Arch. "Cardiaca Vera." Mar. 1935.*

Casey, Kent (pseud. of Kenneth McIntosh). "The Ceres Affair." Oct., 1938.

_____. "Flareback." Mar., 1938.

_____. "Good Old Brig!" July, 1938.

_____. "Melody and Moons." May, 1939.

_____. "Star Crash." Mar., 1939.

_____. "Static." May, 1938.

_____. "They Had Rhythm." Dec., 1938.

_____. "Thundering Peace." Dec., 1939.

Cave, Hugh B. "The Corpse on the Grating." Feb., 1930.
_____. "The Murder Machine." Sept., 1930.
Clark, John D. "Minus Planet." Apr., 1937.*
_____. "Space Blister." Aug., 1937.
Clark, Eddin. "Double! Double!" Sept., 1938.
Coblentz, Stanton A. "The Confession of Dr. DeKalb." Jan., 1934.
_____. "An Episode in Space." May, 1935.
_____. "The Glowworm Flower." June, 1936.
_____. "Gravity, Unaffected." Sept., 1937.
_____. "The Green Plague." Apr., 1934.
_____. "Manna from Mars." Mar., 1934.*
_____. "The Radio Mind Ray." July, 1934.
_____. "The Reign of the Long Tusks." Feb., 1937.
_____. "Riches for Pluto." Dec., 1934.
_____. "Triple-Geared." Apr., 1935.*
_____. "The Truth About the Psycho-Tector." Oct., 1934.*
Coole, Walter Anton. "A Surgical Error." Nov., 1937.
Corbett, Chan (pseud. of Nathan Schachner). "Beyond Infinity." June, 1937.
_____. "Ecce Homo." Jan., 1936.
_____. "Intra-Planetary." Oct., 1935.*
_____. "Nova in Messier 33." May, 1937.
_____. "The Thought Web of Minipar." Nov., 1936.
_____. "When the Sun Dies." Mar., 1935.
_____. "When Time Stood Still." June, 1937.
Cross, Polton (pseud. of John Russell Fearn). "The Degenerates." Feb., 1938.
_____. "The Mental Ultimate." Jan., 1938.
Cummings, Ray. "Beyond the Vanishing Point." Mar., 1931.
_____. *Brigands of the Moon.* 4 pts. Mar.-June, 1930.
_____. *The Exile of Time.* 4 pts. Apr.-July, 1931.*
_____. *Jetta of the Lowlands.* 3 pts. Sept.-Nov., 1930.
_____. "Phantoms of Reality." Jan., 1930.
_____. "An Ultimatum from Mars." Aug., 1939.
_____. "Voyage 13." July, 1938.
_____. "Wandl, the Invader." 2 pts. Feb.-May, 1932.
_____. "The White Invaders." Dec., 1931.
_____. "X1-2-200." Sept., 1938.
Cummins, Dave. "Brain Control." May, 1937.
Curry, Tom. "From an Amber Block." July, 1930.*
_____. "Giants of the Ray." June, 1930.
_____. "Hell's Dimension." Apr., 1931.

_____. "The Soul-Snatcher." Apr., 1930.

Daniels, David R. "Death Cloud." Feb., 1936.

_____. "The Far Way." July, 1935.

_____. "Into the Depths." June, 1935.

_____. "Stars." May, 1935.

_____. "The Way of the Earth." Oct., 1935.

deCamp, L. Sprague. "The Blue Giraffe." Aug., 1939. See also: Lyman R. Lyon (pseudonym).*

_____. "The Command." Oct., 1938.

_____. "Hyperpilosity." Apr., 1938.*

_____. "The Incorrigible." Jan., 1939.

_____. "The Isolinguals." Sept., 1937.

_____. "Living Fossil." Feb., 1939.

_____. "The Merman." Dec., 1938.

del Rey, Lester (pseud. of Ramon F. Alvarez-del Rey). "The Day Is Done." May, 1939.*

_____. "The Faithful." Apr., 1938.

_____. "Habit." Nov., 1939.

_____. "Helen O'Loy." Dec., 1938.*

_____. "The Luck of Ignatz." Aug., 1939.

Diffin, Charles W. *Blue Magic.* 4 pts. Nov., 1935-Feb., 1936. See also: C. D. Willard (pseudonym).

_____. *Brood of the Dark Moon.* 4 pts. Aug.-Nov., 1931.

_____. "Dark Moon." May, 1931.

_____. "The Finding of Haldgren." Apr., 1932.

_____. "The Hammer of Thor." Mar., 1932.

_____. "Holocaust." June, 1931.

_____. "Land of the Lost." 2 pts. Dec., 1933-Jan., 1934.

_____. "The Long Night." May, 1934.

_____. "The Moon Master." June, 1930.

_____. *The Pirate Planet.* 4 pts. Nov., 1930-Feb., 1931.

_____. "The Power and the Glory." July, 1930.*

_____. "Spawn of the Stars." Feb., 1930.

_____. *Two Thousand Miles Below.* 4 pts. June, 1932; Sept., 1932; Nov., 1932; Jan., 1933.

_____. "When the Mountain Came to Miramar." Mar., 1931.

Drew, Douglas. "Nightmare Island." Oct., 1936.*

Duthie, John. "Electrolytic Onslaught." June, 1935.

Edholm, Charlton. "Ping-Ting." Oct., 1933.

Ellis, Sophie Wenzel. "Creatures of the Light." Feb., 1930.

_____. "Slaves of the Dust." Dec., 1930.

Elstar, Dow (pseud. of Raymond Z. Gallun). "Avalanche." Dec., 1935.

_____. "The Second Cataclysm." Mar., 1937.

_____. "Something from Jupiter." Mar., 1938.

_____. "Thunder Voice." Feb., 1938.

_____, and Robert S. McCready. "Stardust Gods." Oct., 1937.

Endersby, Victor. "Disowned." Sept., 1932.

Engelhardt, Frederick (pseud. of L. Ron Hubbard). "General Swamp, C.I.C." 2 pts. Aug.-Sept. 1939.

_____. "This Ship Kills." Nov., 1939.

Ernst, Paul. "From the Wells of the Brain." Oct., 1933.

_____. "Marooned Under the Sea." Sept., 1930.

_____. "Nothing Happens on the Moon." Feb., 1939.

_____. "The Planetoid of Peril." Nov., 1931.

_____. "The Radiant Shell." Jan., 1932.

_____. "The Raid on the Termites." June, 1932.

_____. "The Red Hell of Jupiter." Oct., 1931.

_____. "The Stolen Element." Sept., 1934.

_____. "The Thing in the Pond." June, 1934.

_____. "The 32nd of May." Apr., 1935.*

_____. "The World Behind the Moon." Apr., 1931.

Eshbach, L. A. "The Gray Plague." Nov., 1930.

Evans, Don. "The Last Hope." Sept., 1939.

Farley, Ralph Milne (pseud. of Roger Sherman Hoar), "Black Light." Aug., 1936.

_____. "The Danger from the Deep." Aug., 1931.

_____, and Stanley G. Weinbaum. "Smothered Seas." Jan., 1936.

Fawcett, Col. P. H. "Callahuaya's Curse." Oct., 1933.

Fearn, John Russell. "Before Earth Came." July, 1934. See also: Thornton Ayre, Poulton Cross (pseudonyms).

_____. "The Blue Infinity." Sept., 1935.

_____. "The Brain of Light." May, 1934.*

_____. "Dark Eternity." Dec., 1937.

_____. "Deserted Universe." Sept., 1936.

_____. "Dynasty of the Small." Nov., 1936.

_____. "Earth's Mausoleum." May, 1935.

_____. "He Never Slept." June, 1934.

_____. "The Man Who Stopped the Dust." Mar., 1934.*

_____. "Mathematica." Feb., 1936.

_____. "Mathematica Plus." May, 1936.

_____. "Metamorphosis." June, 1937.

_____. "Red Heritage." Jan., 1938.

_____. "Worlds Within." Mar., 1937.

Fisher, Philip M. "The Lady of the Moon." Sept., 1935.

Flagg, Francis (pseud. of George Henry Weiss). "The Heads of Apex."
    Oct., 1931.
_____. "The Seed of the Toc-Toc Birds." Jan., 1932.
Forman, Jan. "Mr. Ellerbee Transplanted." Oct., 1937.
Frederick, J. George. "The Einstein Express." Apr., 1935.
Gallun, Raymond Z. "A Beast of the Void." Sept., 1936. See also:
    Dow Elstar, E. V. Raymond (pseudonyms).
_____. "Blue Haze on Pluto." June, 1935.
_____. "Buried Moon." Feb., 1936.
_____. "Child of the Stars." Apr., 1936.
_____. "Comet's Captive." June, 1937.
_____. "Davey Jones' Ambassador." Dec., 1935.
_____. "Dawn World Echoes." July, 1937.
_____. "Derelict." Oct., 1935.
_____. "Fires of Genesis." Mar., 1937.
_____. "Godson of Almarlu." Oct., 1936.
_____. "Hotel Cosmos." July, 1938.*
_____. "Iszt—Earthman." Apr., 1938.
_____. "Luminous Mine." Jan., 1937.
_____. "The Machine from Ganymede." Nov., 1934.
_____. "Mad Robot." Mar., 1936.
_____. "Magician of Dream Valley." Oct., 1938.
_____. "Masson's Secret." Sept., 1939.
_____. "A Menace in Miniature." Oct., 1937.
_____. "Mercutian Adventure." Feb., 1938.
_____. "Mind Over Matter." Jan., 1935.*
_____. "N'Goc." May, 1935.
_____. "Old Faithful." Dec., 1934.
_____. "The Path." Nov., 1936.
_____. "The Scarab." Aug., 1936.
_____. "Seeds of the Dusk." May, 1938.
_____. "Shadow of the Veil." Feb., 1939.
_____. "The Son of Old Faithful." July, 1935.
_____. "Space Flotsam." Feb., 1934.
_____. "Telepathic Piracy." Mar., 1935.
_____. "The Wand of Creation." Sept., 1934.
_____. "The Weapon." May, 1936.
_____. "The World Wrecker." June, 1934.
Gee, Jackson. "An Extra Man." Oct., 1930.
Giles, Gordon A. (pseud. of Otto Binder). "Diamond Planetoid."
    May, 1937.
_____. "Wayward World." Feb., 1938.

Gilmore, Anthony (pseud. of Desmond Winter Hall and Harry Bates). "The Affair of the Brains." Mar., 1932.*
_____. "The Bluff of the Hawk." May, 1932.*
_____. "The Coffin Ship." Oct., 1933.
_____. "Four Miles Within." Apr., 1931.
_____. "Hawk Carse." Nov., 1931.*
_____. "The Passing of Ku Sui." Nov., 1932.*
_____. "The Tentacles from Below." Feb., 1931.
Glamis, Walter (pseud. of Nathan Schachner). "The Orange God." Oct., 1933.
Gold, Horace L. "A Matter of Form." Dec., 1938. See also: Clyde Crane Campbell (pseudonym).
_____. "Problem in Murder." Mar., 1939.
Gordon, Peter. "Anything Can Happen!" Oct., 1933.
Graham, Howard W. (pseud. of Howard Wandrei). "Guns of Eternal Day." July, 1934.
_____. "The Other." Dec., 1934.
_____. "Time Haven." Sept., 1934.
_____. "The Wall." May, 1934.
Gregor, Lee (pseud. of Milton A. Rothman). "Heavy Planet." Aug., 1939.*
Guernsey, H. W. (pseud. of Howard Wandrei). "Macklin's Little Friend." Nov., 1936.
Gurwit, S. Gordon. "World Flight." Jan., 1934.
Haggard, J. Harvey. "Denizens of Zeron." Jan., 1937.
_____. "From the Vacuum of Space." Dec., 1937.
_____. "Human Machines." Dec., 1935.
_____. "A Little Green Stone." Mar., 1936.
_____. "Fruit of the Moon Weed." Nov., 1935.
_____. "Lost in Space." Aug., 1935.
_____. "Moon Crystals." Jan., 1936.
_____. "Phantom Star." Oct., 1935.
Hall, Desmond Winter. "Raiders Invisible." Nov., 1931. See also: Anthony Gilmore, H. G. Winter (pseudonyms).
_____. "A Scientist Rises." Nov., 1932.
_____. "Werewolves of War." Feb., 1931.
Hamilton, Edmond. "The Accursed Galaxy." July, 1935.
_____. "The Ephemerae." Dec., 1938.
_____. "Monsters of Mars." Apr., 1931.*
_____. "The Sargasso of Space." Sept., 1931.
_____. "The Second Satellite." Aug., 1930.
Heckman, Royal. "Asteroid Pirates." Aug., 1938.
_____. "The Silver Sphere." Nov., 1938.

Heinlein, Robert. "Life-Line." Aug., 1939.

———. "Misfit." Nov., 1939.

Highstone, H. A. "Frankenstein—Unlimited." Dec., 1936.

Hilliard, A. Rowley. "Breath of the Comet." Jan., 1934.

Holmes, A. R. (pseud. of Harry Bates). "The Slave Ship from Space." July, 1931.

Horn, Holloway. "The Man from Cincinnati." Nov., 1933.

Howard-Burleigh, F. S. "Don MacKinder's Model." Oct., 1933.

Hubbard, L. Ron. "The Dangerous Dimension." July, 1938. See also: Frederick Engelhardt (pseudonym).

———. *The Tramp.* 3 pts. Sept.-Nov., 1938.

Jackson, Stuart. "The Lovely Ghost." Nov., 1933.

James, D. L. "Beyond the Sun." Mar., 1939.

———. "The Cosmo-Trap." Apr., 1936.

———. "Philosophers of Stone." June, 1938.

James, Kenneth. "Burroughs Passes." Oct., 1933.

James, M. F. "The Destruction of Amal." Jan., 1937.

———. "The Expedition from Kytlm." Dec., 1936.

Jameson, Malcolm. "Catalyst Poison." Apr., 1939.

———. "Children of the Betsy-B." Mar., 1939.

———. "Eviction by Isotherm." Aug., 1938.

———. "Mill of the Gods." Jan., 1939.

———. "A Question of Salvage." Oct., 1939.

———. "Seaward." Nov., 1938.

Jenkins, Ainslee. "In the Shadow of the Tii." Nov., 1933.*

Jessel, John (pseud. of Stanley G. Weinbaum). "The Adaptive Ultimate." Nov., 1935.*

Jones, Neil R. "Durna Rangue, Neophyte." June, 1937.

———. "Little Hercules." Sept., 1936.

Keith, Leigh. "No Medals." Mar., 1935.

Kelleam, Joseph E. "Rust." Oct., 1939.*

Kelly, Frank K. "Crater 17, Near Tycho." June, 1934.

———. "Famine on Mars." Sept., 1934.

———. "Star Ship Invincible." Jan., 1935.

Kirby, Jason. "The Floating Island of Madness." Jan., 1933.

Knight, Norman L. "Frontier of the Unknown." 2 pts. June, 1937, Aug., 1937.

———. "Isle of the Golden Swarm." June, 1938.

———. "Saurian Valedictory." Jan., 1939.

Knight, Thomas H. "The Man Who Was Dead." Apr., 1930.

Kostkos, Henry J. "Black Death." Mar., 1934.

———. "The Emperor's Heart." June, 1934.

Kruse, Clifton B. "Code of the Spaceways." July, 1936.
_____. "Dr. Lu-Mie." July, 1934.
_____. "Don Kelz of the I.S.P." Feb., 1936.
_____. "The Drums: An I.S.P. Story." Mar., 1936.
_____. "Flight of the Typhoon." Oct., 1936.
_____. "Fractional Ego." Feb., 1937.
_____. "The Incredible Visitor." May, 1938.
_____. "Menace from Saturn." July, 1935.
_____. "Osa the Killer." Jan., 1935.
_____. "A Princess of Pallis." Oct., 1935.
_____. "The Secret of the Canali." July, 1938.
_____. "A Stranger from Fornalhaut." Jan., 1936.
_____. "The Voice Out of Space." Jan., 1938.
_____. "W-62 to Mercury." Sept., 1935.
_____. "The W-62's Last Flight." May, 1936.
Kummer, Frederick A., Jr. "The Forgiveness of Tenchu Taen." Nov., 1938.
_____. "Lorelei of Space." Feb., 1939.
Kuttner, Henry. "The Disinherited." Aug., 1938.
Lane, Spencer (house pseudonym—unattributed). "Angel in the Dust Bowl." Dec., 1937.
_____. "Niedbalski's Mutant." May, 1938.
_____. "The Origin of Thought." July, 1938.*
Leinster, Murray (pseud. of Will F. Jenkins). "Beyond the Sphinxes' Cave." Nov., 1933.
_____. "The Fourth Dimensional Demonstrator." Dec., 1935.
_____. "The Fifth Dimension Catapult." Jan., 1931.
_____. "The Fifth Dimension Tube." Jan., 1933.
_____. *The Incredible Invasion.* 5 pts. Aug.-Dec., 1936.
_____. "Invasion." Mar., 1933.
_____. "The Mole-Pirate." Nov., 1934.
_____. "Morale." Dec., 1931.
_____. *Murder Madness.* 4 pts. May-Aug., 1930.
_____. "Proxima Centauri." Mar., 1935.
_____. "Sidewise in Time." Apr., 1934.
_____. "Tanks." Jan., 1930.
Leitfred, Robert H. "Prisms of Space." Nov., 1933.
_____. "Prisoners on the Electron." Oct., 1934.
Locke, A. T. "The Machine That Knew Too Much." Dec., 1933.*
_____. "Vandals of the Stars." Mar., 1930.
Long, Amelia Reynolds. "Cosmic Fever." Feb., 1937.
_____. "A Leak in the Fountain of Youth." Aug., 1936.
_____. "The Mind Master." Dec., 1937.

_____. "Reverse Phylogeny." June, 1937.

_____. "Scandal in the 4th Dimension." Feb., 1934.

_____. "When the Half Gods Go." July, 1939.

Long, Frank Belknap. "The Blue Earthman." Apr., 1935.

_____. "Cones." Feb., 1936.

_____. "Exiles of the Stratosphere." July, 1935.

_____. "The Flame Midget." Dec., 1936.

_____. "The Great Cold." Feb., 1935.

_____. "Green Glory." Jan., 1935.*

_____. "The Last Men." Aug., 1934.*

_____. "The Lichen From Eros." Nov., 1935.

_____. "Lost Planet." Nov., 1934.

_____. "Red Storm on Jupiter." May, 1936.

_____. "The Roaring Blot." Mar., 1936.

_____. "Sky Rock." Sept., 1935.

_____. "Spawn of the Red Giants." May, 1937.

_____. "Temporary Warp." Aug., 1937.

_____. "The Vapor Death." Oct., 1934.

Lorraine, Lilith (pseud. of Mary M. Wright). "The Jovian Jest." May, 1930.

Lovecraft, H. P. *At the Mountains of Madness.* 3 pts. Feb.-Apr., 1936.

_____. "The Shadow Out of Time." June, 1936.*

Lyon, Lyman R. (pseud. of L. Sprague deCamp). "Employment." May, 1939.

McClary, Thomas Calvert. "Rebirth." 2 pts. Feb.-Mar., 1934. See also Calvin Peregoy (pseudonym).*

_____. *Three Thousand Years.* 3 pts. Apr.-June, 1938.

MacFadyen, A. "The Endless Chain." Apr., 1937.

_____. "Jason Comes Home." Aug., 1938.

_____. "The Last Selenite." Nov., 1936.

_____. "Space Signals." Dec., 1937.

_____. "The Time Decelerator." July, 1936.

Mason, F.V.W. "Phalanxes of Atlans." 2 pts. Feb.-Mar., 1931.

Meek, S. P. "The Attack from Space." Sept., 1930. See also Sterner St. Paul (pseudonym).

_____. "B.C. 30,000." Apr., 1932.*

_____. "Beyond the Heaviside Layer." July, 1930.

_____. "The Black Lamp." Feb., 1931.

_____. "The Cave of Horror." Jan., 1930.

_____. "Cold Light." Mar., 1930.

_____. "Giants on the Earth." 2 pts. Dec., 1931-Jan., 1932.

_____. "The Great Drought." May, 1932.

_____. "Poisoned Air." Mar., 1932.

Raymond, E. V. (pseud. of Raymond Z. Gallun). "Nova Solis." Dec., 1935.
Raymond, Kaye. "Air Space." Sept., 1937.
_____. "The Comet." Feb., 1937.
_____. "The Great Thought." Mar., 1937.
Rich, H. Thompson. "The Diamond Thunderbolt." July, 1931.
_____. "The Flying City." Aug., 1930.
_____. "Spawn of the Comet." Nov., 1931.
_____. "The Sunken Empire." Jan., 1931.
Rocklynne, Ross. "Anton Moves the Earth." Nov., 1936.
_____. "At the Center of Gravity." June, 1936.
_____. "Jupiter Trap." Aug., 1937.
_____. "Man of Iron." Aug., 1935.
_____. "The Men and the Mirror." July, 1938.
_____. "The Moth." July, 1939.
_____. "Pressure." June, 1939.
_____. "Water for Mars." Apr., 1937.
_____. "Who Was Dilmo Deni?" Nov., 1938.
Rooney, Ray. "The Eye of Madness." Apr., 1937.
Ross, E. L. "Faceted Eyes." Oct., 1935.
Rouse, William Merriam. "The Destroyer." Nov., 1930.
Rousseau, Victor (pseud. of Victor R. Emanuel). "The Atom Smasher."
     May, 1930.
_____. "The Beetle Horde." 2 pts. Jan.-Feb., 1930.
_____. "The Invisible Death." Oct., 1930.
_____. "The Lord of Space." Aug., 1930.
_____. "The Wall of Death." Nov., 1930.
Russell, Eric Frank. "The Great Radio Peril." Apr., 1937.
_____. "Impulse." Sept., 1938.
_____. "Mana." Dec., 1937.
_____. "The Saga of Pelican West." Feb., 1937.
_____, and Leslie T. Johnson. "Seeker of To-Morrow." July, 1937.*
Saari, Oliver E. "The Stellar Exodus." Feb., 1937.
_____. "The Time Bender." Aug., 1937.
_____. "Two Sane Men." June, 1937.
St. John-Loe, G. "Where Four Roads Met." Oct., 1933.
St. Paul, Sterner (pseud. of S. P. Meek). "Into Space." Feb., 1930.
Schachner, Nat. "Ancestral Voices." Dec., 1933. See also Chan Corbett,
     Walter Glamis (pseudonyms).*
_____. "Beyond Which Limits." Feb., 1937.
_____. "City of the Corporate Mind." Dec., 1939.
_____. "City of the Cosmic Rays." July, 1939.
_____. "City of the Rocket Horde." Dec., 1937.

_____. "Crystallized Thought." Aug., 1937.

_____. "Earthspin." June, 1937.

_____. "Entropy." Mar., 1936.

_____. "Eternal Wanderer." Nov., 1936.

_____. "Fire Imps of Vesuvius." Oct., 1933.

_____. "He From Procyon." Apr., 1934.

_____. "I Am Not God." 2 pts. Oct.-Nov., 1935.

_____. "Infra-Universe." 2 pts. Dec., 1936-Jan., 1937.

_____. "Island of the Individualists." May, 1938.

_____. "The Isotope Men." Jan., 1936.

_____. "The Great Thirst." Nov., 1934.

_____. "The Living Equation." Sept., 1934.

_____. "Lost in the Dimensions." Nov., 1937.

_____. "Mind of the World." Mar., 1935.

_____. "Negative Space." Apr., 1938.

_____. "The Orb of Probability," June, 1935.*

_____. "The 100th Generation." May, 1934.*

_____. "Pacifica." July, 1936.

_____. "Palooka from Jupiter." Feb., 1939.

_____. "Past, Present, and Future." Sept., 1937.

_____. "Pirates of the Gorm." May, 1932.

_____. "Redmask of the Outlands." Jan., 1934.

_____. "Return of the Murians." Aug., 1936.

_____. "Reverse Universe." June, 1936.

_____. "The Saprophyte Men of Venus." Oct., 1934.

_____. "The Shining One." May, 1937.

_____. "Simultaneous Worlds." 2 pts. Nov.-Dec., 1938.

_____. "Slaves of Mercury." Sept., 1932.

_____. "The Son of Redmask." Aug., 1935.

_____. "Sterile Planet." July, 1937.

_____. "Stratosphere Towers." Aug., 1934.

_____. "Sunworld of Soldiers." Oct., 1938.

_____. "The Time Imposter." Mar., 1934.

_____. "The Ultimate Metal." Feb., 1935.*

_____. "When the Future Dies." June, 1939.

_____. "Worlds Don't Care." Apr., 1939.

_____, and Arthur Leo Zagat. "The Death Cloud." May, 1931.

_____. "The Revolt of the Machines." July, 1931.

Schere, M. "Anachronistic Optics." Feb., 1938.

_____. "The Brain-Storm Vibration." May, 1938.

_____. "Let Cymbals Ring." Dec., 1938.

Sell, William. "Other Tracks." Oct., 1938.

Sharp, D. D. "Doomed by the Planetoid." Apr., 1936.

———. "The Indesinent Stykal." June, 1937.

Simak, Clifford D. *Cosmic Engineers.* 3 pts. Feb.-Apr., 1939.

———. "Hermit of Mars." June, 1939.

———. "Hellhounds of the Cosmos." June, 1932.*

———. "Hunger Death." Oct., 1938.

———. "Reunion on Ganymede." Nov., 1938.

———. "Rule 18." July, 1938.

Sloat, Edwin K. "Loot of the Void." Sept., 1932.

———. "The Nova." Dec., 1939.

———. "The Space Rover." Feb., 1932.

Smith, Clark Ashton. "The Demon of the Flower." Dec., 1933.*

Smith, E. E. *Galactic Patrol.* 6 pts. Sept., 1937-Feb., 1938.

———. *Gray Lensman.* 4 pts. Oct., 1939-Jan., 1940.

Smith, Will, and R. J. Robbins. "The Soul Master." Mar., 1930.

Sparks, David R. "The Ape-Men of Xlotli." Dec., 1930.

———. "The Winged Men of Orcon." Jan., 1932.

Staley, M. L. "The Stolen Mind." Jan., 1930.

Starr, Paul. "The Invading Blood Stream." Dec., 1933.

Starzl, R. F. "Dimension of the Conquered." Oct., 1934.

———. "The Earthman's Burden." June, 1931.

———. "If the Sun Died." Aug., 1931.

———. "In the Orbit of Saturn." Oct., 1931.

———. "The Martian Cabal." May, 1932.

———. "The Planet of Dread." Aug., 1930.

Stone, Leslie F. (pseud. of Mrs. William Silberberg). "The Great Ones." July, 1937.

Stuart, Don A. (pseud. of John W. Campbell, Jr.). "Atomic Power." Dec., 1934.*

———. "Blindness." Mar., 1935.

———. "Cloak of Aesir." Mar., 1939.

———. "Dead Knowledge." Jan., 1938.

———. "Elimination." May, 1936.

———. "The Escape." May, 1935.

———. "Forgetfulness." June, 1937.

———. "Frictional Losses." July, 1936.

———. "The Invaders." June, 1935.*

———. "The Machine." Feb., 1935.*

———. "Night." Oct., 1935.

———. "Out of Night." Oct., 1937.

———. "Rebellion." Aug., 1935.*

———. "Twilight." Nov., 1934.*

————. "Who Goes There?" Aug., 1938.*

Sturgeon, Theodore. "Ether Breather." Sept., 1939.

Taine, John (pseud. of Eric Temple Bell). *Twelve Eighty-Seven.* 5 pts. May-Aug., 1935.

Taylor, J. Gibson, Jr. "Last Sacrifice." Dec., 1933.

Tench, C. V. "Compensation." Jan., 1930.

Tooker, Richard. "The Green Dome." Dec., 1935.

————. "The Song from the Dark Star." Sept., 1936.

Valding, Victor (pseud. of John Victor Peterson). "Atmospherics." Sept., 1939.

Van Campen, Karl (pseud. of John W. Campbell, Jr.). "The Irrelevant." Dec., 1934.

Van Lorne, Warner (pseud. of Nelson Tremaine). "Austrolano." July, 1936.

————. "Blue Men of Yrano." Jan., 1939.

————. "Desert City." Mar., 1937.

————. "Follow the Robot Trail." Sept., 1936.

————. "Glagula." June, 1936.

————. "Liquid Power." July, 1935.

————. "Marinorro." Nov., 1937.

————. "Ormoly of Roonerion." Jan., 1938.

————. "Other Space." May, 1937.

————. "Resilient Planet." Aug., 1938.

————. "Strange City." Jan., 1936.

————. "Vibratory." Mar., 1938.*

————. "White Adventure." Apr., 1936.

————. "Winter on the Planet." Apr., 1937.

————. "World of Purple Light." Dec., 1936.

Van Lorne, Warner (pseud. of F. Orlin Tremaine—this story only). "The Upper Level Road." Aug., 1935.*

Van Vogt, A. E. "Black Destroyer." July, 1939.*

————. "Discord in Scarlet." Dec., 1939.

Vincent, Harl (pseud. of Harold Vincent Schoepflin). "The Copper-Clad World." Sept., 1931.

————. "Cosmic Rhythm." Oct., 1934.

————. "Creatures of Vibration." Jan., 1932.

————. "Energy." Jan., 1935.

————. "Gray Denim." Dec., 1930.

————. "Lost City of Mars." Feb., 1934.

————. "The Moon Weed." Aug., 1931.

————. "The Morons." June, 1939.

————. "Old Crompton's Secret." Feb., 1930.

_____. "The Plane Compass." June, 1935.

_____. "Power Plant." Nov., 1939.

_____. "Prowler of the Wastelands." Apr., 1935.

_____. "Return of the Prowler." Nov., 1938.

_____. "Rex." June, 1934.*

_____. "Silver Dome." Aug., 1930.

_____. "Telegraph Plateau." Nov., 1933.

_____. "The Terror of Air Level Six." July, 1930.

_____. "Terrors Unseen." Mar., 1931.

_____. "Vagabonds of Space." Nov., 1930.

_____. "Vulcan's Workshop." June, 1932.

_____. "Wanderer of Infinity." Mar., 1933.

Von Drey, Howard (pseud. of Howard Wandrei). "The God Box." Apr., 1934.

Walton, Harry. "Below—Absolute." June, 1938.

_____. "The Cache." Apr., 1939.

_____. "Episode on Dhee Minor." Oct., 1939.

_____. "Quicksilver, Unlimited," July, 1937.

Wandrei, Donald. "The Atom-Smasher." Spr., 1934.

_____. "Blinding Shadows." May, 1934.

_____. "Collossus." Jan., 1934.

_____. "Collossus Eternal." Dec., 1934.

_____. "Earth—Minus." Sept., 1935.

_____. "Farewell to Earth." Dec., 1933.

_____. "Finality, Unlimited." Sept., 1936.

_____. "Infinity Zero." Oct., 1936.

_____. "Life-Current." Apr., 1935.

_____. "The Man Who Never Lived." Mar., 1934.

_____. "Murray's Light." June, 1935.*

_____. "The Nerveless Man." July, 1934.

_____. "A Race Through Time." Oct., 1933.

_____. "Raiders of the Universes." Sept., 1932.

_____. "A Scientist Divides." Sept., 1934.*

_____. "The Whisperers." May, 1935.

Weinbaum, Stanley G. "Flight on Titan." Jan., 1935. See also John Jessel (pseudonym).

_____. "The Lotus Eaters." Apr., 1935.

_____. "The Mad Moon." Dec., 1935.

_____. "The Parasite Planet." Feb., 1935.*

_____. "The Planet of Doubt." Oct., 1935.

_____. "Proteus Island." Aug., 1936.

_____. "The Red Peri." Nov., 1935.

_____. "Redemption Cairn." Mar., 1936.
Wellman, Manly Wade. "Forces Must Balance." Sept., 1939.
_____. "Men Against the Stars." June, 1938.
_____. "Nuisance Value." 2 pts. Dec., 1938-Jan., 1939.
_____. "Outlaws on Callisto." Apr., 1936.
_____. "Pithecanthropus Rejectus." Jan., 1938.
_____. "Rule of the Bee." Oct., 1937.
_____. "Treasure Asteroid." Sept., 1938.
_____. "Wings of the Storm." Mar., 1938.
Wells, Hal K. "The Cavern of the Shining Ones." Nov., 1932.
_____. "Devil Crystals of Arret." Sept., 1931.
_____. "The Gate to Xoran." Jan., 1931.
_____. "The Purple Brain." Dec., 1933.
_____. "When the Moon Turned Green." May, 1931.
_____. "Zehru of Xollar." Feb., 1932.
Wernham, Guy. "Outcasts." Nov., 1934.
West, Wallace (pseud. of George Wallace West). "Dragon's Teeth."
    Sept., 1934.
_____. "En Route to Pluto." Aug., 1936.
_____. "The End of Time." Mar., 1933.
_____. "The Phantom Dictator." Aug., 1935.
_____. "Plane People." Nov., 1933.
_____. "The Retreat from Utopia." Mar., 1934.
_____. "Sculptors of Life." Dec., 1939.
Willard, C. D. (pseud. of Charles Willard Diffin). "The Eye of Allah."
    Jan., 1931.
_____. "Out of the Dreadful Depths." June, 1930.
Willey, Robert (pseud. of Willy Ley). "At the Perihelion." Feb., 1937.
_____. "Orbit XXIII-H." Sept., 1938.
Williams, Robert Moore. "Flight of the Dawn Star." Mar., 1938. See
    also Robert Moore (pseudonym).
_____. "Robot's Return." Sept., 1938.*
Williamson, Jack. "The Blue Spot." 2 pts. Jan.-Feb., 1937.
_____. "Born of the Sun." Mar., 1934.*
_____. *The Cometeers.* 4 pts. May-Aug., 1936.
_____. "Crucible of Power." Feb., 1939.
_____. "Dead Star Station." Nov., 1933.
_____. "The Doom from Planet 4." July, 1931.
_____. "The Flame from Mars." Jan., 1934.
_____. "The Galactic Circle." Aug., 1935.
_____. "Islands of the Sun." 2 pts. Sept.-Oct., 1935.
_____. "The Lake of Light." Apr., 1931.

_____. *The Legion of Space.* 5 pts. Apr.-Sept., 1934.

_____. *The Legion of Time.* 3 pts. May-July, 1938.

_____. "The Meteor Girl." Mar., 1931.

_____. *One Against the Legion.* 3 pts. Apr.-June, 1939.

_____. "The Pygmy Planet." Feb., 1932.

_____. "Released Entropy." 2 pts. Aug.-Sept., 1937.

_____. "Salvage in Space." Mar., 1933.

_____. "Terror Out of Time." Dec., 1933.

Wilson, Robert H. "Out Around Rigel." Dec., 1931.

Winter, H. G. (pseud. of Harry Bates and Desmond Winter Hall). "The Hands of Aten." July, 1931.

_____. "The Midget from the Island." Aug., 1931.

_____. "Seed of the Arctic Ice." Feb., 1932.

_____. "Under Arctic Ice." Jan., 1933.

Winterbotham, R. R. "Clouds Over Uranus." Mar., 1937.

_____. "Einleill." July, 1937.

_____. "The Fourth Dynasty." Dec., 1936.

_____. "Linked Worlds." Jan., 1937.

_____. "Procession of Suns." May, 1938.

_____. "The Psycho Power Conquest." Feb., 1936.

_____. "The Secret of the Rocks." Dec., 1937.

_____. "Specialization." Aug., 1937.

_____. "Spore Trappers." May, 1937.

_____. "The Star That Would Not Behave." Aug., 1935.

_____. "The Train That Vanished." July, 1936.

Wire, Don. "Oil." Feb., 1939.

Woodbury, David O. "Aground in Space." Aug., 1934.

_____. "The Electric Snare." July, 1934.

Wright, Sewell Peaslee. "The Dark Side of Antri." Jan., 1931.

_____. "The Death Traps of FX-31." Mar., 1933.

_____. "The Forbidden Planet." July, 1930.

_____. "From the Ocean's Depths." Mar., 1930.

_____. "The Ghost World." Apr., 1931.

_____. "The God in the Box." Sept., 1931.

_____. "The Infra-Medians." Dec., 1931.

_____. "Into the Ocean's Depths." May, 1930.

_____. "The Man from 2071." June, 1931.

_____. "Priestess of the Flame." June, 1932.

_____. "The Terrible Tentacles of L-472." Sept., 1930.

_____. "The Terror from the Depths." Nov., 1931.

_____. "Vampires of Space." Mar., 1932.

Wycoff, J. Earle. "The Seeing Blindness." Feb., 1936.

Zagat, Arthur Leo. "Beyond the Spectrum." Aug., 1934.
_____. "The Great Dome on Mercury." Apr., 1932.
_____. "The Living Flame." Feb., 1934.
_____. "Spoor of the Bat." July, 1934.
_____. "When the Sleepers Woke." Nov., 1932.
Ziska, K. F. "Man of Ages." Oct., 1934.
_____. "Succubus." May, 1934.

Bibliography

PRIMARY SOURCES

Recent Anthologies of "Pulp" Science Fiction

Ashley, Michael. *The History of the Science Fiction Magazine; Vol. 1: 1926-1935.* 1974; rpt. Chicago: Regnery, 1976.

———. *The History of the Science Fiction Magazine; Vol. 2: 1936-1945.* 1975; rpt. Chicago: Regnery, 1976.

———. *The History of the Science Fiction Magazine; Vol. 3: 1946-1955.* Chicago: Contemporary Books, 1977.

Asimov, Isaac, ed. *Before the Golden Age: A Science Fiction Anthology of the 1930's.* New York: Doubleday, 1974.

Goodstone, Tony. *The Pulps: 50 Years of American Pop Culture.* New York: Chelsea House, 1976.

Knight, Damon Francis, ed. *Science Fiction of the Thirties.* 1975; rpt. New York: Avon, 1977.

Fiction from the 1930s

Astounding Science Fiction. March, 1938 to December, 1939. (See Appendix.)

Astounding Stories. Published monthly from January, 1930 to February, 1938, except for July, August, October, December, 1932; February, 1933; April-September, 1933. (See Appendix).

Campbell, John W. "The Black Star Passes." *Amazing Stories Quarterly,* Fall 1930, pp. 492-523; 574.

———. "The Last Evolution." *Amazing Stories,* Aug. 1932, pp. 414-21.

Hamilton, Edmond. "The Island of Unreason." *Wonder Stories,* May 1932, pp. 970-77.

Manning, Laurence. "The Elixir" (Part V of *The Man Who Awoke*). *Wonder Stories,* Aug. 1933, pp. 150-59; 183-85.

Moore, C. L. "Shambleau." *Weird Tales,* Nov. 1933. Rpt. in *The Best of C. L. Moore.* Ed. Lester del Rey. New York: Ballantine, 1975, pp. 1-32.

Stone, Leslie F. (pseud.). "The Conquest of Gola." *Wonder Stories,* Apr. 1931, pp. 1278-87.

Fiction Outside the 1930s

Andrevon, J. P. "Observation of Quadragnes." Trans. Frank Zero. In *View From Another Shore.* Ed. Franz Rottensteiner. New York: Seabury, 1973, pp. 61-82.

Bunch, David. *Moderan.* New York: Avon, 1971.

Capek, Karel. *R.U.R.* Trans. P. Selver. 1923; rpt. New York: Washington Square Press, 1969.

Conan Doyle, Sir Arthur. *The Poison Belt.* 1913; rpt. New York: Berkley, 1961.

Disch, Thomas. "Fun With Your New Head." In *Under Compulsion.* London: Granada, 1970, pp. 128-29.

Finney, Jack. *The Body Snatchers.* New York: Dell, 1955.

LeGuin, Ursula K. *The Left Hand of Darkness.* New York: Ace, 1969.

Lem, Stanislaw. "The Eighth Voyage." Trans. Michael Kandel. In *The Star Diaries.* 1971; rpt. New York: Avon, 1977, pp. 23-44.

––––––. "Prince Ferrix and the Princess Crystal." Trans. Michael Kandel. In *The Cyberiad.* 1971; rpt. New York: Avon, 1976, pp. 227-36.

Strugatsky, Arkady, and Boris Strugatsky. "Spontaneous Reflex." Trans. Violet L. Dutt. In *Soviet Science Fiction.* Ed. Isaac Asimov. New York: Collier Books, 1962, pp. 89-111.

Varley, John. "The Persistence of Vision." In *The Persistence of Vision.* New York: Dial, 1978, pp. 226-72.

Wells, H. G. *Seven Science Fiction Novels of H. G. Wells.* 1934; rpt. New York: Dover, n.d.

Wister, Owen. *The Virginian.* 1902; rpt. New York: Pocket Books, 1974.

MAGAZINE HISTORY

Early Assessments (1926-1945)

"Amazing! Astounding!" *Time,* 10 July 1939, p. 32.

"A Penny A Word." *American Mercury,* Mar. 1936, pp. 285-92.

Barclay, Alvin. "Magazines for Morons." *The New Republic,* 28 Aug. 1929, p. 42.

"Big Business in Pulp Thrillers: Love and Adventure Stories Gross $25,000 a Year." *Literary Digest,* 23 Jan. 1937, p. 30.

Gibbs, Angela. "Onward and Upward With the Arts: Inertium, Neutronium, Chromalogy, P-P-P-Proot!" *New Yorker,* 13 Feb. 1943, pp. 42-53.

Hersey, Harold. *Pulpwood Editor: The Fabulous World of the Thriller Magazine Revealed by a Veteran Editor and Publisher.* New York: Frederick A. Stokes, 1937.

Huxley, Aldous. "Pulp." *Saturday Review of Literature,* 17 July 1937, pp. 10-11.

Jones, Archer. "The Pulps—A Mirror to Yearning." *North American Review,* 246, No. 1 (Autumn 1938), 35-47.

MacMullen, Margaret. "Pulps and Confessions." *Harper's Magazine,* 175 (June 1937), 94-102.

Pratt, Fletcher, "The Pulp Magazines." *Saturday Review of Literature,* 3 July 1937, pp. 3-4.

Robinson, Henry Morton. "The Wood-Pulp Racket." *Bookman,* 67 (Aug. 1928), 648-51.

Uzzell, Thomas. "The Love Pulps." *Scribner's,* 103 (Apr. 1938), 36-41.

Recent Assessments (1955-1980)

Ashley, Michael. "An Amazing Experiment." In *The History of the Science Fiction Magazine; Vol. 1: 1926-1935.* Ed. Michael Ashley. *1974; rpt. Chicago: Regnery, 1976, pp. 11-51.*

————. "Introduction: SF Bandwaggon." In *The History of the Science Fiction Magazine; Vol. 2: 1936-1945.* Ed. Michael Ashley. 1975; *rpt. Chicago: Regnery, 1976, pp. 11-76.*

Beaumont, Charles. "The Bloody Pulps." *Playboy,* Sept. 1962. Rpt. in *The Fantastic Pulps.* Ed. Peter Haining. New York: Vintage, 1976, pp. 397-414.

Blackbeard, Bill. "The Pulps." In *Handbook of American Popular Culture.* Ed. Thomas Inge. Westport, Conn.: Greenwood Press, 1978, pp. 195-223.

Goulart, Ron. *An Informal History of the Pulp Magazine.* 1972; rpt. *New York: Ace Books, 1973.*

Gruber, Frank. *Pulp Jungle.* New York: Sherbourne Press, 1967.

Jones, Robert Kenneth. *The Shudder Pulps: A History of the Weird Menace Magazines of the 1930s.* West Linn, Oregon: FAX Collector's Editions, 1975.

Peterson, Theodore. *Magazines in the Twentieth Century.* Urbana, Ill.: Univ. of Illinois Press, 1956.

Reynolds, Quentin James. *The Fiction Factory, or From Pulp Row to Quality Street: The Story of 100 Years of Publishing at Street and Smith.* New York: Random House, 1955.

FAN HISTORY

Friend, Beverly. "The Science Fiction Fan Cult." Diss. Northwestern Univ. 1974.

Knight, Damon. *The Futurians: The Story of the Great Science Fiction "Family" of the 30's That Produced Today's Top Writers and Editors.* New York: John Day, 1977.

Moskowitz, Sam. *The Immortal Storm: A History of Science Fiction Fandom.* 1954; rpt. Westport, Conn.: Hyperion Press, 1974.

Rogers, Alva. *A Requiem for* Astounding. Chicago: Advent, 1964.

Warner, Harry J. *All Our Yesterdays: An Informal History of Science Fiction Fandom in the Forties.* Chicago: Advent, 1969.

THEORY AND CRITICISM

Books and Anthologies

Aldiss, Brian W. *Billion Year Spree: The True History of Science Fiction.* 1973; rpt. New York: Schocken, 1974.

Carter, Paul. *The Creation of Tomorrow: Fifty Years of Magazine Science Fiction.* New York: Columbia Univ. Press, 1977.

Cawelti, John G. *Adventure, Mystery, and Romance: Formula Stories As Art and Popular Culture.* Chicago: Univ. of Chicago Press, 1976.

Clareson, Thomas. *Voices of the Future.* Bowling Green, Ohio: Bowling Green Popular Press, 1976.

Franklin, H. Bruce. *Future Perfect: American Science Fiction of the Nineteenth Century.* New York: Oxford Univ. Press, 1966.

Hirsch, Walter. "American Science Fiction 1926-50: A Content Analysis." Diss. Northwestern Univ. 1957.

Johnson, William, ed. *Focus on the Science Fiction Film.* Englewood Cliffs, N.J.: Prentice-Hall, 1972.

Ketterer, David. *New Worlds for Old: The Apocalyptic Imagination, Science Fiction, and American Literature.* Bloomington, Ind.: Indiana Univ. Press, 1974.

Mogen, David Lee. "Frontier Themes in Science Fiction." Diss. Univ. of Colorado 1977.

Moskowitz, Sam. *Seekers of Tomorrow: Masters of Modern Science Fiction.* New York: Ballantine Books, 1967.

_____. *Under the Moons of Mars.* New York: Holt, Rinehart, and Winston, 1970.

Parrinder, Patrick. *Science Fiction: Its Criticism and Teaching.* London: Methuen, 1981.

Randall, David A., Sigmund Casey Fredericks, and Tim Mitchell. *An Exhibition on Science Fiction and Fantasy.* Bloomington, Ind.: Univ. Office of Publications, 1975.

Rose, Mark. *Alien Encounters: Anatomy of Science Fiction.* Cambridge, Mass.: Harvard University Press, 1981.

Scholes, Robert. *Structural Fabulation: An Essay on Fiction of the Future.* Notre Dame, Ind.: Univ. of Notre Dame Press, 1975.

_____, and Eric S. Rabkin. *Science Fiction: History—Science—Vision.* New York: Oxford Univ. Press, 1977.

Suvin, Darko. *The Metamorphoses of Science Fiction: On the Poetics and History of a Literary Genre.* New Haven: Yale Univ. Press, 1979.

Treguboff, Zoe. "A Study of the Social Criticism in Popular Fiction: A Content Analysis of Science Fiction." Diss. UCLA 1955.

Warrick, Patricia. *The Cybernetic Imagination in Science Fiction.* Cambridge, Mass.: MIT Press, 1980.

Wolfe, Gary K. *The Known and the Unknown: The Iconography of Science Fiction.* Kent, Ohio: Kent State Univ. Press, 1979.

Articles and Reviews

Baring-Gould, W. S. "Little Superman, What Now?" *Harper's,* Sept. 1946, pp. 283-88.

Budrys, Algis. "Paradise Charted." *TriQuarterly,* 49 (Fall 1980), 4-75.

DeVoto, Bernard. "Doom Beyond Jupiter." *Harper's,* Sept. 1939, pp. 445-48.

Honeycutt, Kirk. "Director of 'Alien' Launches Cold Terror Into Outer Space." *Minneapolis Star,* 25 June 1979, Sec C, p. 1, cols. 3-6.

Johnson, Glen. " 'We'd Fight . . . We Had To': *The Body Snatchers* as Novel and Film." *Journal of Popular Culture,* 13 (Summer 1979), 5-16.

Samuelson, David. "The Spinning Galaxy: A Shift in Perspective on Magazine Science Fiction." *Extrapolation,* 17, No. 1 (Dec. 1975), 44-48.

Sapiro, Leland. "The Mystic Renaissance: A Survey of F. Orlin Tremaine's *Astounding Stories.*" *Riverside Quarterly,* 2 (June 1966), 75-88; 2 (Nov. 1966), 156-70; 2 (Mar. 1967), 270-83.

VISUALS

Gerani, Gary, and Paul H. Schulman. *Fantastic Television: A Pictorial History of Sci-Fi, The Unusual, and The Fantastic.* New York: Harmony Books, 1977.

Giger, H. R. "H. R. Giger's Alien Encounters." *Penthouse,* April 1980, pp. 142-53.

Kaufman, Philip, dir. *Invasion of the Body Snatchers.* With Leonard Nimoy and Donald Sutherland. United Artists, 1978.

Nyby, Christian, dir. *The Thing (From Another World)*. With James
    Arness. RKO, 1951.
Scott, Ridley, dir. *Alien*. With Sigourney Weaver and Ian Holm. Twentieth
    Century Fox, 1979.
Siegel, Don, dir. *Invasion of the Body Snatchers*. With Kevin McCarthy.
    Allied Artists, 1956.

BIBLIOGRAPHIES

Barron, Neil, ed. *Anatomy of Wonder: Science Fiction*. New York: R. R.
    Bowker, 1976.
Day, Donald B. *Index to the Science Fiction Magazines 1926-50*. Portland,
    Oregon: Perri Press, 1953.
Resnick, Michael. *The Official Guide to the Fantastics*. Florence,
    Alabama: House of Collectibles, 1976.
Rock, James A. *Who Goes There: A Bibliographic Dictionary of
    Pseudonymous Literature in the Fields of Fantasy and Science
    Fiction*. Bloomington, Ind.: James A. Rock and Co., 1979.

OTHER

Historical Statistics of the United States, Part 1. Washington, D.C.:
    U.S. Dept. of Commerce, 1975.
Statistical Abstract of the United States: 1977. Washington, D.C.:
    U.S. Dept. of Commerce, 1977.

Index

About the Author

FRANK L. CIOFFI is Assistant Professor of English at Eastern New Mexico University. His writings have appeared in *Extrapolation*, the *Journal of English Teaching Techniques*, and other publications.